Paul and Denise Burton

walk & eat
around LISBON

walk & eat LISBON

PLAN OF CENTRAL LISBON	*inside front cover*
INTRODUCTION	4
the walks	6
the excursions	7
AUTHORS' NOTE	7
the restaurants	8
the recipes	9
portuguese food	10
portuguese wines	10
planning your visit	12
when to go	12
where to stay	13
what to take	14
planning your walks	15
on arrival	17
tourist information	17
city transport pass	12
shopping for self-catering	19
markets	19
WALK 1 • lisbon city	20
alternative visits: belém, parque das nações	31
restaurant: comida da ribeira	31
recipes: salt cod brás-style, *leite-crème*	32
WALK 2 • sintra castles and palaces	34
restaurant: restaurante regional de sintra	43
recipes: goan-style curry, coriander soup with poached egg	44
WALK 3 • monserrate and capuchos	46
restaurants: café de paris, sintra	51
recipes: chicken breast stuffed with spinach and nuts, marinated horse-mackerel	52
WALK 4 • peninha circuit from azóia	54
restaurants: pão de trigo, azóia	60
recipe: turbot and prawn kebab	61

CONTENTS

contents

WALK 5 • azenhas do mar 62
restaurants: ribeirinha de colares, restaurante da várzea,
 azenhas do mar 70
recipes: rabbit stew, prawn bread soup 72

WALK 6 • westward to cabo da roca 74
restaurant: casa da galé, praia grande 82
recipe: pork with clams, Alentejo-style 75

WALK 7 • arrábida peninsula 84
restaurant: restaurante bombordo, setúbal 90
recipes: *rodizio de peixe*, orange roll 91

WALK 8 • sado's rice paddies 92
restaurants: museu do arroz and ilha do arroz, comporta 100
recipes: razor-shell and cockle rice, sweet rice pudding,
 duck rice, cockles *bulhão pato*-style 102

WALK 9 • cabo espichel 106
restaurant: i love espichel 116
recipe: drunken pears 117

WALK 10 • lourinhã's dinosaurs 118
restaurant: restaurante foz 126
recipe: fish stew 127

EXCURSION 1 • alcochete 128
restaurant: solar do peixe, alcochete 131

EXCURSION 2 • óbidos 132
COSTA DE LISBOA AREA MAP 134
restaurants: cozinha das rainhas, ilustre casa de ramiro 135

CHOOSING BACALHAU 136

EAT GF, DF 138
eating in restaurants 138
self-catering 139
 gf, df shopping 139

TRANSPORT 135

GLOSSARY (menu decoder, shopping items, conversion table) 140

INDEX 143

IN THE RESTAURANT (pocket vocabulary) ..... *inside back cover*

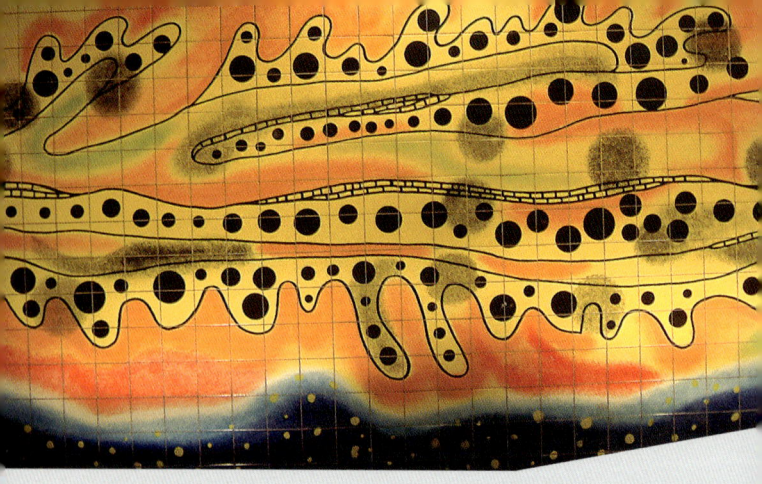

This pocket guide is designed for short-break walking holidays from Lisbon, using the excellent public transport network (or a car, if you prefer). Fly out for just a week or a long weekend. You have in your hand enough walks, excursions, restaurants and recipes to last two weeks — so you can pick and choose the most appealing.

The highlights at a glance:
- 10 varied day walks, each with topographical map
- 2 excursions — one to the Tagus Estuary Natural Park, the other to the medieval walled town of Óbidos
- recommended restaurants for the walks and excursions
- recipes to make at your self-catering base or back home
- special section with hints on wheat-, gluten- and dairy-free eating and cooking in the Lisbon area

INTRO

introduction

There is little doubt that Lisbon has risen significantly in the European capital popularity stakes in recent decades, and deservedly so! Hosting Expo98 and the 2004 European Football Championship helped enormously, not only in promoting the city as an attractive destination, but also as catalysts in improving tourist infrastructures. Travelling within the city and to the surrounding areas, whether by public or private transport, has been made immeasurably more visitor-friendly as a direct result of hosting these major events.

Building on this, our book does not attempt to be a general guide to the city itself — there are many of these — instead, we provide practical information on using Lisbon as a base for walking and eating in the wider 'Costa de Lisboa' (Lisbon Coast) region.

Extending from Peniche in the north to Sesimbra and Setúbal in the south and to the River Tagus in the east, the **Costa de Lisboa**, linked geographically and commercially to Lisbon, offers a wonderful variety of scenery, culture and an insight into the rich heritage of Portuguese history.

The pre-historical presence of dinosaurs near Lourinhã and at Cabo Espichel, the early Phoenician use of Lisbon as a port of call on their trading routes north, the Roman occupation of Lisbon, followed by the Moors, their conquest in 1147 and finally the establishment of Lisbon as capital of Portugal in 1255, are all events that have left their mark — from fossils to archaeological remains to the imposing Castelo São Jorge in Lisbon and Moors' Castle in Sintra.

But it doesn't end there; with the establishment of Portugal as a nation, this landscape became indelibly marked by the hand of man through the colourful events of national history. Medieval towns like Óbidos (Excursion 2) and the establishment of Sintra (Walk 2) as a place of retreat from Lisbon — these and many more have influenced the landscape, architecture and way of life we see today.

THE WALKS

There are walks in this book for everyone; from easy, generally flat routes to moderate upland hikes. They have been chosen because they can be *easily reached by public transport from Lisbon and because they offer good eating en route*. In addition, the walks attempt to offer variety of scenery and interest; some following a specific theme — such as dinosaurs at Lourinhã and Cabo Espichel or rice production in the Sado Estuary.

Padrão dos Descobrimentos, Belém

> **Authors' Note**
> Much has changed in the twenty years that have passed since we prepared the first edition of this book. The new motorways, housing and tourist developments all signs of growing prosperity and the ever-increasing pressure on the countryside around Lisbon.
>
> There have been few major changes since preparing the Second edition six years ago, but a couple of routes have been altered because the land came into private ownerhip. We have also updated some details, particularly relating to travel within the area.
>
> The restaurants are mostly unchanged, a reflection of their consistent quality and of the continuing Portuguese love for and pride in their traditional cuisine which is gaining deserved recognition internationally.
>
> In recent years the Portuguese have taken to outdoor pursuits as never before, amongst which and not least is walking. This in turn has led to a much greater awareness and appreciation of the natural environment as well as a growth in the number of waymarked walks.

THE EXCURSIONS

We have suggested two 'day out' excursions from Lisbon. One takes you by ferry across the Tagus Estuary to Montijo, where you join the bus service to Alcochete, the gateway to the Tagus Estuary Natural Park. Enjoy seeing flamingos and other birdlife from the Interpretation Centre, returning to Lisbon after lunch.

The second is a bus ride north to the beautiful medieval town of Óbidos. When you see it you will understand why for centuries Portuguese kings offered the town as a wedding gift to their brides. Not only does Óbidos preserve its architectural integrity almost perfectly, but it also offers plenty of good restaurants.

THE RESTAURANTS

Based on personal experience, we have recommended at least one restaurant for each walk and excursion. As well as a description of the restaurant, we give a typical summary menu, highlighting their specialities where appropriate. A price guide is given (€ to €€€), to indicate 'very reasonable' to 'fairly pricey'. But remember that you can have a relatively inexpensive meal in quite 'up market' establishments by selecting the *prato do dia* (dish of the day) or the *ementa turistica* (tourist menu), topped off with *vinho de casa* (house wine). Frequently a light lunch taken in this way can cost less than €18 per person.

Rainbows of fish — the mainstay of the Portuguese diet

Eating out in the evenings is generally more expensive, as there is usually no *prato do dia* available. It is also worth remembering that many restaurants will serve you half-portions *(meia dose)* if you ask; indeed, in Portugal full portions can often be daunting and will put paid to post-lunch walking!

Remember that by law all restaurants are supposed to remain closed for at least one day of the week. We have indicated wherever possible which day this was at the time of writing. *No restaurant has paid — in cash or kind — to be included in this guide.* Our choice is based strictly on personal taste and experience; inclusion (or exclusion) should be so interpreted.

THE RECIPES

The recipes selected from the menus of the various restaurants we feature have been chosen to offer as wide a spectrum of dishes as possible. Being near the coast, almost all restaurants feature fresh fish prominently. But in order to achieve an *overall balance* in the recipes, we will describe one of the restaurant's meat dishes, even though they clearly specialise in fish. Rest assured that they *do* also serve meat. If specific dishes we mention are not on the menu, this is because chefs retire or move on …

> **Cookery books**
>
> *Lisboeta: Recipes from Portugal's City of Light* by Nuno Mendes (ISBN 978-14088-770-12)
>
> *The Taste of Portugal* by Edite Vieira (ISBN 978-1911-6211-88) — a voyage of gastronmic discovery combined with recipes.
>
> *Portuguese Cooking* (ISBN 88-476-0921-6) — a well-illustrated introduction to regional dishes, with a background history
>
> *Eat Portugal* (ISBN 978-929-23-3133-1)

Restaurant staff, and chefs in particular, are nearly always ready and happy to talk about their food and its preparation. There is, however, an understandable reluctance to divulge every last secret of how a dish is prepared. We have gathered as much information as possible and then built on this by cooking the dishes — often more than once — at home, to ensure that they are workable. This has proved to be a considerable challenge for Denise who, being a vegetarian, has suddenly had to face preparing a whole host of meat dishes which she would not normally have contemplated!

Sunflower's request for special consideration to be given to readers with food intolerances was another hurdle, but we hope our recipes — all of which can be made **gluten- and dairy-free** (see page 139) will be of real help and enable them to enjoy to the full their excursions and walks with us.

PORTUGUESE FOOD

Portuguese food is a wonderful mix of the Mediterranean and Atlantic, both in terms of the contrasting fish and shellfish and the produce from the land itself, which 'hovers' between these two ecosystems. Moreover there is often the hint of Africa, Brazil or the Orient in the cooking, due partly to historical links but also, and especially around Lisbon, the more recent influx of migrant workers.

Apart from *bacalhau* (dried cod; see page 136) and **smoked meat** (sausages, hams, etc), nearly all Portuguese cooking relies heavily on **good fresh produce**. The market gardens to the north (seen, for example, on Walk 10) are testimony to this, as are the well-stocked markets of Lisbon. Fresh **fish** and **shellfish** are also available in incredible variety and abundance.

With the passage of time it becomes more difficult to identify which dishes truly originated in Lisbon as opposed to other parts of the country. Certainly *bacalhau à Brás* (see page 32) is a Lisbon creation, as is *amêijoas à Bulhão Pato* (see page 105). But many dishes served in and around Lisbon are available throughout Portugal, and their true geographic origin is lost in history.

Central to Portuguese cooking is olive oil. Portuguese 'azeite' has improved enormously and now regularly wins top international awards. The health benefits of Extra Virgin Olive Oil (EVOO) are well known. Portuguese EVOOs, just like wines, have distinctive regional flavours — those from the Trás-os-Montes being more robust and quite different from those originating in the Alentejo. You can expect a good EVOO to be piquant and even cause you to cough!

PORTUGUESE WINES

To complement a meal, whether in a restaurant or in self-catering, Portuguese wines offer an amazing choice. Many of the better wines are still relatively unknown outside Portugal, so a restaurant wine list or supermarket shelf may look quite bewildering, with few recognisable names.

The Costa de Lisboa to the north and west of the Tagus produces the **Estremadura Regional Wines** ('Vinho Regional' on the label). Within this region there are specific Demarcated (sub)Regions ('VPQRD' on the label), such as Lourinhã, Óbidos, Alenquer, Torres Vedras, Bucelas and Colares. As a general rule, the VPQRD wines tend to be

Try these!

Wines from Estremadura
- Quinta de Abrigada Tinto (DOC)
- Valle do Riacho Tinto or Branco (VQPRD)
- Tinta Roriz Tinto
- Aba da Serra Tinto

Colares
Casal de Azenha tinto — particularly good value

Bucelas
Quinta do Avelar

Glossary
DOC: wine from a demarcated region;
VPQRD: quality wine from a demarcated sub-region;
Regional: wine from a DOC area, but not using recognised grapes;
garrafa: bottle;
rolha: cork (in case you want to take it home!)

Tip: A highly readable account of Portuguese wine (with an excellent historical section that encompasses much more than just viniculture), *The Wines and Vineyards of Portugal* by Richard Mayson (Mitchell Beazley, 2003) is not to be missed.

made predominantly with *national* grape varieties, while the Regional wines frequently contain some of the better-known *international* grape varieties blended in.

Apart from the better-known white *(branco)* wines from Bucelas (25km north of Lisbon) and the small remaining production of red *(tinto)* from Colares, the Estremaduran wines have begun to receive attention only relatively recently. Many producers have significantly improved quality, and there are some excellent wines now available from this little-known region.

To the south of the Tagus lies the 'Terras do Sado' wine region, within which is the Setúbal sub-region (with the longest history of wine production in Iberia), famous for its Moscatel de Setúbal, a sweet fortified wine.

Wines to look out for from further afield include the (generally) *lighter reds* from the Douro (Esteva, Evel, Tuella, Dorna Velha, Duas Quintas) or the much *heavier reds* from the Alentejo (Borba, Esporão, Mouchão). For *whites* try Planalto (Douro), João Pires (Palmela/Alentejo) or, from the far north, an Alvarinho *vinho verde*.

PLANNING YOUR VISIT
When to go
Lisbon is worth visiting at any time of the year, but winter (especially November to March) can be foggy, misty and rainy. This is not a great problem for visiting the city itself (or enjoying some of our restaurants), but is likely to make walking in the surrounding countryside less enjoyable. Even so, there can be

fine, sunny spells throughout the winter, although these are difficult to predict.

Most Lisboetas go on holiday in August, and while there is far less traffic congestion in the city itself, nearby coastal resorts such as Cascais and Estoril can be very crowded.

For walking probably the best time of year is **spring/early summer** (April to June). The weather is generally good, and the temperatures not too high. Above all, the countryside is most vividly coloured at this time.

Autumn, too, is good for walking, but days become shorter and, beyond mid-October, the weather can be unpredictable.

Averages	**Jan**	**Feb**	**Mar**	**Apr**	**May**	**Jun**
Temperature (°C)	11	12	14	15	17	20
Rainfall (mm)	95	87	85	60	46	18
Averages	**Jul**	**Aug**	**Sep**	**Oct**	**Nov**	**Dec**
Temperature (°C)	22	23	22	19	15	12
Rainfall (mm)	4	5	33	75	100	97

Where to stay

Lisbon has a huge selection of accommodation from luxury hotels to humble *residençias.* For easy access via public transport to the walks described in this book, choose accommodation near the **city centre**. An alternative, if you only intend doing the walks to the north of Lisbon, might be to stay at **Sintra**, which has good public transport links to most of the walks. If you have your own transport, you could well consider staying in one of the excellent *Turismo Rural* properties outside Lisbon.

Alternatively you might like to try self-catering accommodation. There's plenty available; just search 'Lisbon apartment rental' on the internet and you will get a wealth of ideas. Then you'll be able to try some of our recipes using local ingredients!

What to take

Pack simply! Eating out in Portugal, even for dinner, is generally fairly informal, and the restaurants we list are no exception — so apart from some smart casuals, concentrate on packing appropriate walking gear.

While no special equipment is needed for any of the walks, proper **walking boots** are preferable to any other footwear. Many walks can become slippery when wet, and some are on uneven surfaces with loose gravel, so good ankle support is essential. Paths often have large puddles and can become streams during or after rain, so good walking boots will help keep your feet dry. Each person should carry a **small rucksack**, and *all year round* it is advisable to pack it with a **sunhat, first-aid kit, spare socks** and some **warm clothing**. A **long-sleeved shirt** and **long trousers** should be worn or carried, for sun protection and for pushing your way through encroaching vegetation (which may be wet and prickly). You should always carry a **smart/mobile phone**; the **emergency** number in Portugal (as throughout the EU) is **112**. At least one member of the party should carry a **compass** (or **GPS**), and a pair of **compact binoculars** can often be helpful in spotting distant waymarks (as well as birdlife and dinosaur prints!).

Depending on the season, you may also need a **windproof**,

lightweight rainwear, fleece and **gloves**. Optional items include **swimwear** and a **Swiss Army Knife** (packed in your hold luggage, not hand luggage, or it will be confiscated!). Mineral water is sold almost everywhere in plastic half or one-and-a-half litre bottles; *it is imperative that each walker carries at least half a litre of water — a full litre or more in summer*.

If you are self-catering and enjoy your 'cuppa', you may find it worth bringing your own **tea bags**; they are available locally but often of indifferent quality. Don't forget to pack a **UK-to-Continental plug adapter** and all the **battery chargers** you need!

Planning your walks

Look through the walk descriptions in advance; this will help you decide if any additional equipment might be required. The walks are specifically designed for access by the local and regional bus and rail network … so that you can enjoy a bottle of wine with lunch! But if you do want to hire a car, and the route is linear, you can usually leave your car at the end of the walk and then take a bus to the start. Bear in mind that if you are driving and are tempted to imbibe at lunchtime, the **local alcohol limit is 0.5mg/l**, significantly lower than in the UK. Police carry out random checks and, if you are involved in an accident, you will automatically be breathalysed.

The walks have been **graded** for level of difficulty, but none of them should be beyond the capabilities of anyone who takes moderate and regular exercise. The maximum height gain on any of the walks is 350m, but gradients are generally pretty gentle; any exceptions are specifically mentioned. It is wise to remember that the times indicated are *neat point-to-point and do not allow for any stops;* you should **allow up to double the time shown** to take into account photo and refreshment stops.

The **walking maps** are based on Openstreetmap mapping, annotated from our notes and GPS work in the field. We have checked them against our GPS readings and found them very accurate. Moreover, free **GPS track** downloads are available for all these walks: see the *Walk & eat around Lisbon* page on the Sunflower website. *Even if you don't use GPS,* these maps are so accurate that you can easily compare them with Google Maps on your smartphone and pinpoint your exact position. The most useful printed maps you can buy are the 1:25,000 'Carta Militar' M888 Series published by the Instituto Geográfico do Exército: see sheet numbers in the info panels for each walk.

Walking safely depends in great part on knowing what to expect and being properly equipped. For this reason we urge you to *read through the whole walk description* at your leisure before setting out, so that you have a mental picture of each stage of the route and the landmarks. Some of the walks have been waymarked usually with red/yellow stripes (= means this way, X means not this way, ⌈ means turn right and ⌉ turn left). But beware: waymarking is often poor or confusing, so *always follow our route description or refer to our GPS downloads.*

Some of the walks do penetrate quite isolated countryside, and none of them is likely to be busy with other walkers (except in the Sintra hills at weekends). It may be quite a while before anyone finds you if you get into difficulty, so our advice is: **never walk alone**.

ON ARRIVAL

Tourist information

Lisbon Airport is very close to the centre of town. In addition to a metro station at the airport, there are airport buses to the city centre and plenty of taxis (make sure the meter is set!).

There are **tourist information desks** in the arrivals area of the airport, one for Lisbon and another for the whole of Portugal. The main tourist office is in Praça dos Restauradores (1 on the plan inside the front cover), but for really comprehensive information on Lisbon, you should go to the **Lisboa Welcome Centre** in the Praça do Comércio (2 on the plan).

Train times can be obtained from Santa Apolónia station (300m off the east side of the plan) or at **www.cp.pt** .

All towns have their own tourist information offices from which you will usually be able to get a town plan and tips on any local sites or sights of interest. The major tourist attractions (Sintra, Cabo de Roca, etc) also have information offices.

City transport pass

For travel **within Lisbon**, a 'Lisboa Card', valid for 1, 2 or 3 days gives you unlimited travel on the bus and metro services together with entry to many museums and monuments. This, as well as suburban rail services to Sinta and Cascais, is available at airport arrivals, Santa Apolónia station, the Welcome Centre or online. For full details see **www.lisboacard.org**. There is also a rechargable 'Navegante' card for transport only: find details on the web.

walk & eat LISBON

Mercado da Ribeira

For the **Sintra area**, Carris Metropolitan bus services provide connections to Cascais as well as local services. Both Lisboa and Navegante cards can be used on Carris.

For journey planning go to **www.transporlis.pt**.

Shopping for self-catering

If you are daunted by the Portuguese language, then clearly the answer to shopping, as anywhere, is to head to one of the big 'self-serve' **hypermarkets**. Lisbon has several such shopping centres, and they generally offer excellent quality food in great variety — including fresh fish and shellfish, a great variety of meats, deli counters and bakeries.

These shopping centres also have *natural produce and special diet shops* — for example at the **Centro Comercial Colombo** (Colégio Militar metro station) or **Centro Comercial Vasco da Gama** (Oriente metro station). If you are looking for specialist health foods, however, then head for one of the 13 branches of Celeiro (see page 139).

Markets

For the more adventurous, a visit to the **local market** is *the* way to do your shopping. To help, we have prepared a shopping vocabulary (page 141). Best known is the (Time Out) **Mercado da Ribeira**, just west of Cais do Sodré station (600 m west of the Praça do Comércio), described in more detail on page 31. But you'll find other food markets dotted around the city.

This walk introduces some of Lisbon's essential characteristics and history. It leads from the planned layout of Pombal's Baixa up through older streets to the Castelo São Jorge, dating from the time of the Visigoths and Moors. From this remarkable viewpoint you descend through the confusion of Alfama's steep, narrow alleys to Praça do Comércio, where Lisbon meets the Tagus.

lisbon city
WALK

Start the walk at the **Estação do Rossio** (3 on the plan). From the front of the building walk over to the beflagged national theatre (**Teatro Dona Maria II;** 4) on your left and then to the fountain in the **Praça Dom Pedro IV**. Cross the square towards the Rossio metro station opposite and go through the adjacent **Praça da Figueira** just beyond it, from where the statue of **Dom João I** (5) makes an imposing foreground to the Castelo São Jorge crowning the hilltop (photo opposite).

Distance: 6km/3.7mi plus time at the castle and grounds; allow 4-6h; see plan inside front cover

Grade: easy-moderate; there are some steep climbs up towards Santa Luzia and the castle (overall ups and downs of 190m/625ft), but you can always 'cheat' if it's too hot by catching the number 28 tram from Praça da Figueira up to Santa Luzia.

Equipment: comfortable walking shoes

Transport: 🚌 or 🚋 to the Estação do Rossio

Refreshments en route: throughout

Opening hours:
Castelo São Jorge (main fortifications) 09.00-18.00 daily (21.00 from Mar-Oct); paid

Keeping to the left of the statue, leave the square on the north side along Rua Dom Duarte (later Rua da Palma). Curve right, rounding the Hotel Mundial on your right, then turn left along **Praça Martim Moniz**, skirting the right-hand side of the eponymous square — a rather soulless, largely modern open space. After some 100 metres you will come to the church of **Senhora da Saúde** (6). The fairly simple exterior conceals some beautiful blue and white tiles inside, so it's well worth taking a look.

On leaving the church, walk back down Rua da Mouraria for about 25 metres and then turn left by the pharmacy to take the

Escadinhas da Saúde ('Little Stairway of Health'). It's a pretty steep climb — good for your health! — but there are strategically placed benches if you want to have a breather on the way.

On reaching Rua Marquês de Ponte de Lima turn right and, now on the level, you will come to Largo da Rosa where, on the corner, you will find an old convent and the church of **São Lourenço** (7). Turn left and immediately ahead of you are steps leading up towards the castle (Escadinha do Castelo). But instead of taking these, turn right into Rua das Farinhas, dropping gently into Largo de São Cristovão, where you will come to the church of **São Cristovão** (8). Walk in front of the church and then climb Calçada Conde Marquês Tancos up to the left, past **Chão do Loureiro** (9) on your right, a multi-story car park with a rooftop viewpoint and café-restaurant. It's also an 'art gallery'; each floor has been decorated by the country's top street artists. Just next door, past the ZamBeZe Restaurant, you can pause on a little terrace for more views out across the city.

Continuing ahead, you will see the 'Chapitos' Acção Social building: pass this and, about 25 metres further on, take the Escadinhas de São Crispim down to the right, passing the **Irish College** (1611; 10 on the plan), which survived the great Lisbon earthquake of 1755. At the bottom, turn right along Rua São Mamede, then take the second left turn, down Travessa do Almada. This will bring you steeply down to the church of **Santa Maria Madalena** (11).

From here follow the tramlines to the left uphill along Rua Santo António da Sé, passing the church of **Santo António** (12) on the left and immediately after, on the next bend, the imposing **Sé** (cathedral; 13 on the plan). Walk to the left of the cathedral, still following the tram lines. You pass the **Museu do Aljube** (14) on your left — a museum dedicated to the struggle against fascism housed in the old prison where dissidents were held during Salazar's long dictatorship. Finally you you will have climbed high enough to emerge at the **belvedere** by the church of **Santa Luzia** (15).

Tile mural at the Santa Luzia belvedere and and the charming urinal at Travessa Funil

Notice the fine tile murals both on the church and the belvedere itself, the latter depicting old Lisbon as seen from the river. This is a very pleasant spot to sit for a while and recover from the climb. You can look over the city and to the wide expanse of the Tagus beyond — and down on the mosaics of daily life carrying on in the Alfama district below you.

Opposite Santa Luzia you will see the Travessa da Santa Luzia: follow this up through a small square (Largo do Contador Mor) and continue up Travessa Funil — at the top of which is a charming public urinal. Turn left along Chão da Feira: ahead of you now is the outer entrance to **Castelo de São Jorge** (16 on the plan) and the old residential area surrounding

In the grounds of Castelo São Jorge

the castle itself. As you pass through, notice the shrine to São Jorge on your left. Just above, on the right, is a Welcome Centre, where you can pick up a detailed map of the castle and buy your entrance ticket. A little further up is the Governor's House, which has quite a good selection of books for sale.

You now come to the entrance to the main fortifications, and you can easily spend an hour wandering around in this area, with its wonderful mix of trees, stone columns, statues, old arches and cannons pointing out over the city. The views on all sides are superb. There is an up-market restaurant here, as well as a less expensive cafeteria serving light snacks.

After your visit, retrace your steps to the main entrance; just outside there is a bus stop, should you want to catch transport back down to the city centre.

To continue the walk, turn right along Travessa São Bartolomeu, then left in front of the sports centre. Wind your way back down to Largo do Contador Mor and the church of Santa Luzia. Turn left, following the tram lines to just past the church, where you come to a small **viewpoint and café** (17 on the plan; Largo das Portas do Sol). From here you can take in the views across Alfama, the church of **São Vicente** (18; burial place for the House of Bragança monarchs) and the church of **Santa Engrácia** (19) — the National Pantheon which houses, among others, the tombs of Prince Henry the Navigator, Luís Camões and Vasco da Gama.

Return to just by the corner of Santa Luzia Church, then follow the steep stairway (Rua Norberto de Araujo/later Rua da Adiça) down past a small vine-shrouded fountain to Rua São

Casa dos Bicos: this Renaissance palace (1523) is named for the unusual pointed stones *(bicos)* on the façade. The 1755 earthquake destroyed the two top floors, which were not repaired until the 1980s. Exhibitions are sometimes held here.

João da Praça. Turn left here and, after passing through Largo São Rafael, take Rua São Miguel on the left: this brings you shortly to the church of **São Miguel** (20) in a lovely little square dominated by a fine palm tree.

Continue on along Rua São Miguel until you come to another small square at a T-junction. Turn right here on Rua da Reguiera but, almost immediately, take the narrow flight of steps up to the left (Beco Carneiro). Turning right at the top, you pass a lovely old fountain on your left. Turn up left just after this and you will come up to the church of **Santo Estevão** (21). Turn right here along Rua Santo Estevão, to a small square with a children's playground, where you join Rua Vigário. Turn right at once which bring you immediately into Rua dos Remédios, where you turn right.

You come down to the **Museu do Fado** (22) and the Largo do Chafariz de Dentro. Carry on along Rua Terreiro do Trigo, passing the **Chafariz d'el Rei** (King's Fountain; 23) and the **Casa dos Bicos** (24), before finally coming into Campo das

Arcaded ministerial buildings in the Praça do Comércio, dating from the rebuilding of the city after the earthquake by the Marqués de Pombal

Cebolas. Carry on into Rua Alfândega, passing the **door of Nossa Senhora da Conceição** (25) — the only part of this church to survive the 1755 earthquake.

Continue following the tramlines, to arrive in the magnificent **Praça do Comércio** (2), once the main maritime gate to the city. Thankfully this is no longer used as a car park: you can walk around the central expanse and really appreciate the beautiful symmetry, with various ministerial buildings occupying three sides and the Tagus the fourth. Walk under the main archway into Rua Augusta; there are plenty of snack bars and restaurants in the streets off either side.

When you reach the junction where Rua Santa Justa crosses pedestrianised Rua Augusta, turn left to come to the iconic tower housing the **Elevador de Santa Justa** (26). If the queue is not too long, ride to the top, from where you will get fine views back over to Castelo São Jorge and down to the Praça Dom Pedro IV below. When you come back down, as you leave the lift, just turn up left along Rua Aurea and back to the **Estação de Rossio** (3).

Estação Oriente, Parque das Nações

Alternative visits

To see a few of the famous riverside sites and monuments, arm yourself with a large-scale free city plan or a general guidebook and take the metro to **Cais do Sodré** (600 metres west of 2 on the plan). Then hop on a tram out to Belém (but beware, this tram route — and the bus equivalent — is notorious for pick-pockets). Then just stroll around the **Jerónimos Monastery**, the modern **Belém Cultural Centre** and the **Torre de Belém**. You may be tempted to walk back along the riverfront, but this is a disappointing option, as you frequently have to divert back to the busy and noisy Avenida da India.

A better idea is to get the tram (or bus) back as far as the **Doca de Santo Amaro** just by the suspension bridge, **Ponte 25 de Abril**. Here you will find a wonderful selection of restaurants, with cuisine from all over the world, in the old warehouses located in front of what is now a yacht marina.

For a complete contrast to the 'historical' monuments, which no visitor to Lisbon should miss, be sure to take in the supermodern **Parque das Nações** (the Expo98 site). It's almost worth going there just for the metro trip — to see the stunning modern *azulejos* (wall tiles) that adorn the stations on the way. On arrival at Oriente, the Parque das Nações metro station, you will come out into the splendid **Oriente** railway station. Walk up onto the

Torre de Belém, with the 25 Abril suspension bridge in the background

mainline platforms to really appreciate the elegant use of steel by the Spanish architect, Santiago Calatrava, who designed it.

Unlike some other Expo sites, Lisbon's has been a great post-Expo success. This more or less derelict area of the city has been transformed into a vibrant community. The shopping centres are always busy, and there are plenty of restaurants and good hotels. And of course, there are the main buildings from Expo still to be seen; not least the **Oceanarium** (the largest in Europe), the **Portugal Pavilion** and the enormous **Altice Arena** (now used for hosting major indoor events such as masters tennis). The backdrop is the imposing 17km-long **Ponte Vasco da Gama**, built to coincide with Expo98.

walk & eat LISBON

Praça Dom Pedro IV and the Café Nicola

There are countless restaurants and snack bars along the route of the walk and alternative visits. For best value, just drop into one of the small restaurants (if it looks busy with locals you can be confident of good food) at about lunch time on any weekday and ask for the *prato do dia* or *diario*. Usually there will be a set lunch-time menu which will include soup, main course and sweet

restaurants

eat

> **TIME OUT MARKET LISBOA**
> Av 24 de Julho, 49 (Mercado)
> ☏ 213 951 274
> www.timeoutmarket.com
> Sun-Wed 10am to midnight; Thu-Sat 10am to 2am €-€€€
>
> a choice of **24 restaurants** — everything from steaks to Portuguese specialities like *bacalhau* and *leite-crème* (see recipes overleaf), sushi, pizza, suckling pig, burgers, fusion, organic soups and salads …
>
> **8 bars**: beers, wines, champagnes
>
> **12 speciality kiosks** — from herbs to port wine, liquors and Portuguese chocolates
>
> **the concept** is to present the very best of food/top chefs from around Lisbon — to whet your appetite, go to www.timeoutmarket.com/lisboa/en/eat-and-drink
>
> **live music some evenings**

(sometimes also coffee and wine). This all-inclusive meal can cost as little as €9.

We mention the **Mercado da Ribeira** on page 19 as a good spot to buy fresh produce for self-catering. This was the city's main market from 1892 until 2014 and a landmark in the Cais do Sodré area, with its oriental dome and iron interior. The main market has now been moved to the north of the city (São Julião do Tojal), and the Mercado da Ribeira only handles retail sales. A huge restaurant on the ground floor is run by the Lisbon team of *Time Out* magazine.

Time Out Market Lisboa

In the west wing of the Mercado da Ribeira, *Time Out* magazine runs a food court with almost 50 restaurants, bars and kiosks selling speciality products. It's *very* busy and noisy — a fun place to go for a quick bite or to visit with a convivial group, definitely *not* a venue for a quiet meal! You choose the food yourself, then take your seat at one of the long wooden tables (there are 750 places) or on the terrace. Prices are noticeably higher than elsewhere, but this is a place to experience at least once — 'a gastronomic orgy' according to satisfied visitors. Live music too!

Salt cod Brás-style *(bacalhau à Brás)*

Soak the cod fish in fresh water for 24 hours, changing the water several times (see the special section on *bacalhau* on page 136). Skin the fish and take out the bones. Shred the fish into small pieces.

Cut the potatoes into stick-like chips, the onions into fine rings and finely chop the cloves of garlic. Fry the potatoes in hot oil until they brown slightly, then drain on kitchen paper.

In a heavy-based saucepan, gently fry the onion and garlic until the onion is soft. Then add the shredded cod fish (with a tablespoon of Madeira).

Ingredients (for 4 people)

- 400 g *bacalhau* (salted cod fish)
- 3 tbsp olive oil
- 500 g potatoes
- 6 eggs, lightly beaten and seasoned with salt and pepper
- 3 onions
- 2 cloves of garlic
- tbsp Madeira wine
- parsley
- cooking oil for frying the potato chips
- black olives
- cooked prawns (optional, as shown above)

Add the fried potato chips to the fish mixture, then the seasoned eggs. Stir the mixture with a fork until it becomes creamy and cooked. Put onto a serving dish and sprinkle with chopped parsley. Garnish with black olives and/or the boiled prawns if you wish.

recipes

eat

Leite-crème (a crème brûlée)

This recipe might prove a little difficult to do in a rented apartment unless you go out and buy a *ferro,* a small iron plate with a handle which can be heated up on the gas. Otherwise, this is one to try at home, when you can get the blowtorch out of the tool shed!

Beat the egg yolks with the caster sugar, flour and a little milk. Sieve the mixture and slowly add the rest of the milk and the lemon peel.

Cook gently on a low heat, stirring all the time. When the mixture begins to boil, turn down the heat and simmer for 2 minutes, stirring continuously. Remove the lemon peel and pour the mixture into a shallow dish or individual dishes and leave to cool.

Before serving sprinkle sugar on the crème and scorch, using by placing a hot *ferro* on top or using a cook's blowtorch — one of those gadgets now fairly widely available and handy for making crème brûlée and browning toppings on other dishes.

Salt cod Bras-style (opposite) and *leite-crème* (below), as served at Time Out Market

Ingredients (for 4 people)
0.5 l milk
100 g caster sugar
4 egg yolks
1 tbsp flour
1 lemon (peel only)
sugar to sprinkle

Our walk takes you from the historic centre of Sintra all the way up to the castle, Pena Palace and on to Cruz Alta. The whole of the walk is within the area designated a UNESCO World Heritage Site in 1995. As you follow in our footsteps, you will appreciate the reasons for this classification.

sintra castles and palaces
WALK

sintra castles and palaces walk 2

Sintra is little more than half an hour from Lisbon but has a totally different atmosphere. The town itself is made up of three parts: the old historic centre, the 'village' of São Pedro, and the more modern area (Estefânia). Most visitors head straight for the historic centre, by the Palácio Nacional, although Estefânia sees its share of visitors for the fortnightly second-hand market.

The Sintra Hills rise up to their highest point at Cruz Alta (528m) and consist of syenitic and granitic rocks intruded into the lower-lying and surrounding limestone. Being so near the coast, the hills experience the full force of Atlantic wind and rain in winter. This explains the dense vegetation and tree cover (although the exposed western end has little); the climate encouraged past generations to introduce many foreign species of shrubs and trees in the gardens around their country houses.

Distance: 7.6km/4.7mi; 2h06min

Grade: moderate, with ascents/descents of 350m/1150ft overall. Generally good under foot on gravel pathways; plenty of shade. *IGE 1:25,000 M888 Series map, sheet 416*

Equipment: see pages 14-15

Transport: 🚆 from Lisbon to Sintra (very frequent; see page 142), then walk 0.5km to the old centre, or take a hop-on, hop-off 🚌. Or 🚗 to Sintra (38° 47.905'N, 9° 23.197'W)

Refreshments en route:
Sintra and tea house at Pena Palace

Opening times/Prices
All are closed 25/12 and 1/1; www.parquesdesintra.pt. You need a ticket to enter the park; consider buying a combination ticket with access to the palaces and castle. Concessions.
Sintra National Palace daily; 09.30-19.00 (mar-nov 18.00); €13
Pena National Palace daily; apr-oct 09.45-19.00; nov-mar 10.00-18.00; €17 (includes **gardens**)
Queluz National Palace daily; 09.30-19.00 (mar-nov 18.00); €11
Castelo dos Mouros daily; apr-oct 09.30-20.00; nov-mar 10.00-18.00; €10.20

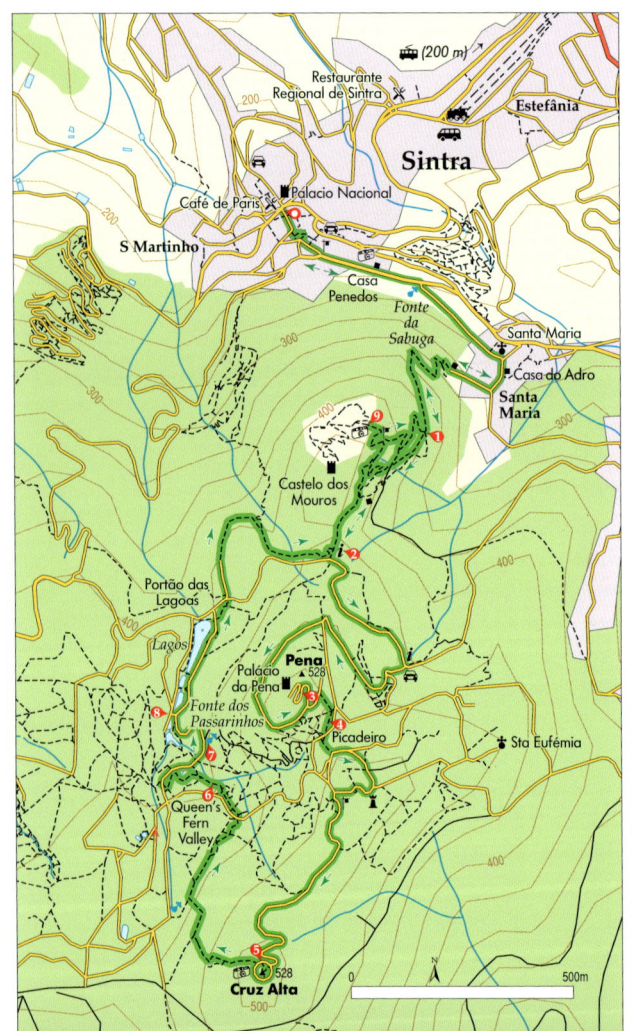

Wherever you are in Sintra, you will see signs of its historical popularity with monarchs and nobility as a place of retreat from the summer heat of Lisbon. Apart from the grand 'formal' palaces there are many smaller *palacetes* and follies dotted around the hillside, many with quite exquisite architecture, some quite bizarre!

Sintra was also a favourite with many well known names, including Hans Christian Andersen, Graham Greene, Richard Strauss, William Beckford and Lord Byron.

Byron first arrived in Lisbon by sea in July 1809:

'What beauties doth Lisboa first unfold!

Her image floating on that noble tide.'

Just two verses after the above lines in Childe Harold, he penned the following immortal words:

Lo! Cintra's glorious Eden intervenes

In variegated maze of mount and glen.

Ah, me! What hand can pencil guide, or pen,

To follow half on which the eye dilates

Through views more dazzling unto mortal ken

Although some 200 years have passed, there is enough of that original ambience and attraction today. It's well worth spending time in the old town (preferably avoiding the busy weekends), which is full of cafés, restaurants and shops offering antiques and handicrafts. But always above you are the hills, and atop the hills the Moors' Castle and Pena Palace. Even at night their floodlit presence is felt, often mysteriously wrapped in fast-moving mist or fog.

Begin the walk in the main square (**Largo da Raina Dona Amélia**; ⦿) opposite the Café Paris Restaurant (179m). Walk up Rua das Padarias and, on the first bend, take steps up left to the **Arca Ferreirinha**. Once through this arch, turn right up more steps, following yellow and red waymarks and coming to signposts for PR1 and PR3 (**2min**). Turn left following the PR1 sign towards 'Igreja Santa Maria'. Pass the **Casa Penedos** on your left (from where there are fine views down to the National Palace) and come to the **Fonte da Sabuga** on your right (**5min**). Turn up right on cobbles (Calcada dos Clérigos) to the **Igreja Santa Maria** (**9min**). From the church walk up past **Casa do Adro** (where Hans Christian Andersen stayed in 1866) and, a minute later, turn right up the steep **Rampa do Castelo**

The path levels out as you walk below the Moors' Castle (18min)

(ignoring the 'X' waymark), passing the **Forestry Department office** on the right.

The cobbles give way to steps and a dirt track which brings you to a narrow revolving **gate** — the entrance to the grounds surrounding the Moors' Castle (❶; **13min**). Zigzag up to the right just 10 metres above the gate and, ignoring the steps up to the

The Lagos

right (**18min**; your return route), follow the main, level path. But a minute later *do* fork right uphill (above a small castellated house). When the path swings round to the right (**20min**), ignore steps off to the left. A minute later, turn sharp left at a junction with a blue 'P' (for 'parking') sign; the way ahead leads to the Moors' Castle, but first you need an entrance ticket (unless you've already bought one online). Walk through another revolving gate (**24min**) and on to the **Visitor Centre** (❷). Here you should buy tickets to enter the Moors' Castle (on your return later in the walk) and Pena Palace gardens (as well as the palace itself, if you wish to go inside). Turn left along the road past the Visitor Centre and descend to a car park and another **Visitor Centre** (**28min**). Turn in through the gates (showing your ticket) and follow a well-marked road up to **Pena Palace** (❸; 487m; **40min**).

After visiting the palace, return down to the pill-box just a minute below and turn left down a road. In two minutes turn

Pena Palace

right on a path, to come to the open space at the **Picadeiro** (**❹**; **44min**). Walk through this riding arena to the opposite corner and take the footpath up to the left (ignoring the road ahead under a bridge). In another half minute you rise to a roughly surfaced track; turn left and in another half minute fork right, to walk below the **Statue of the Giant** (or **Warrior**), perched on rocks. Walk round to the right of the statue, then turn left at the major junction (**47min**), coming immediately to a sign for 'Cruz Alta'.

Wind up the road to **Cruz Alta** (**❺**; 528m; **57min**). Where the road divides, just below the summit, keep left, then take the steps up to the viewpoint. Return down the same steps and, when you rejoin the road, turn right. After almost completely circling this high point and just before another flight of steps up to the viewpoint, go through a break in the wall on the left, to find a couple more steps leading down to a steep narrow footpath.

Follow this down through dense woodland and, at a junction (**1h10min**) keep right downhill. At the next, T-junction, turn right (**1h14min**). In another minute you will come down to a **fountain and water tank**, just beyond which you join a dirt trail. Turn right here, now on the level. At a junction after only 20 metres, keep right. Then, about 80 metres further on, at another junction with two trails off left (**1h21min**), take the second one, going steeply downhill for a minute, to a road. Cross the road and walk into the **Queen's Fern Valley** (**6**). Various paths lead down through this beautiful verdant valley; it doesn't matter which one you take — just keep downhill. Coming out to a road again, turn right to the Moorish **Fonte dos Passarinhos** (**7**).

Sintra National Palace with twin chimneys rising above the kitchens

On leaving this fountain, walk down left on tarmac, following the 'Lagos' sign. At the **Lagos** (lakes; **8**; **1h26min**) look out for the resident black swans and grey herons as you continue downhill, now following signs to the **Portão das Lagoas** (gateway; **1h28min**). Cross the main road up to the right and go through the gate opposite (by another blue 'P' sign). Follow the trail, then path, round and below **Pena Palace** to

A somewhat irreverent tile decoration for a café-bar in Sintra — even angels can be tempted here!

Queijadas de Sintra

Many Portuguese towns have their own 'speciality' cake. Sintra is no exception, and the *queijadas de Sintra* (Sintra cheesecakes) have a fame which goes well beyond the town itself.

Like most Portuguese pastries, they are quite sweet, the ingredients being soft sheep's milk cheese, sugar, flour, eggs and cinnamon. Several shops sell *queijadas*, but the most famous are probably those sold at the always-busy **Piriquita** bakery — just across the road from Café de Paris (by the start of this walk).

emerge back at the **Visitor Centre** (❷; **1h37min**). Retrace your outward route to the first junction with the blue 'P' sign and now keep ahead to another junction, where you turn left (past a ruined church and displays of local archaeological finds) up to the entrance to the **Castelo dos Mouros** (Moors' Castle; ❾; 435m; **1h42min**). Show your ticket, go through the gate and explore the grounds inside the castle walls. On clear days there are spectacular views down to Sintra, back to Pena Palace, and to the coast beyond.

Leaving the castle, retrace your steps to the church ruins just below the entrance, where you follow the sign for the GR11 footpath. This will bring you back down to the 18min-point of the outward route in six minutes. Retrace your steps back down to the old centre of **Sintra** (❶; **2h06min**, *not including* visits!).

Sintra is a very popular attraction for visitors the whole year round, its proximity to Lisbon and its World Heritage status providing good reasons for a day out from the capital. Not surprisingly, a vigorous hotel and restaurant trade has developed in response to tourist demands. In fact you can eat out in splendour at Queluz National Palace, stay overnight in the Seteais Palace or choose from many other excellent hotels and restaurants in and around the town.

We have selected just a couple of restaurants, one for this walk and another for Walk 3, but do not regard our choice as in any way exclusive!

For this walk we have chosen the small **Restaurante Regional de Sintra**, a rather old-fashioned restaurant tucked away behind Sintra's Town Hall, halfway between the old centre and the railway station. The clientèle is mostly local, the staff very helpful and friendly, and the restaurant is pleasantly decorated with tile murals (see overleaf). The menu is available in English.

RESTAURANTE REGIONAL DE SINTRA
Travessa do Município 2, Sintra
(219 234 444; www.regional.pt
Daily ex Wed €€

good choice of **starters**, including several traditional soups, like *canja* (chicken broth), *açorda à Alentejana* (coriander soup with poached egg; recipe on page 45).

plenty of **fish and seafood** dishes, choose either plain grilled fish or try a *caldeirada de mariscos* (seafood stew) or *caril de gambas* (prawn curry; recipe on page 44).

meat dishes include steaks done in several different ways, pork, chicken and lamb

for **sweets** there is an ice-cream menu and home-made dishes including chocolate mousse, mulberry profitarolles, Molotov pudding (a creation of beaten egg whites with a rich egg yolk sauce) or a selection of fresh fruit.

---

restaurants

eat

Goan-style curry *(caril de gambas)*

Wash the prawns and cook them in salted boiling water for 2 minutes. Drain and cool in cold water, then remove the heads and shells.

Heat the butter in a saucepan, add chopped onion, apple and pineapple and cook until soft. Stir in the flour until well blended, then add the curry powder and cook for a few minutes. Gradually stir in the coconut milk and milk, add seasoning as required and bring to the boil.

Lower the heat and cook for 15-20 minutes, stirring occasionally. If the mixture becomes too thick, add a little more milk. Remove from the heat, cool, then put the mixture in a blender until smooth. Return the blended ingredients to the saucepan, add the peeled and shelled prawns and heat through.

Serve on a bed of plain boiled rice, sprinkle the prawns with desiccated coconut, and garnish with slices of fresh fruit — perhaps apple, banana, kiwi and grapes.

Ingredients (for 4 people)

1 kg raw prawns
1 onion, chopped
1 apple, chopped
2 pineapple rings, chopped
1 tbsp flour
1 tbsp curry powder
50 g butter
200 ml coconut milk
400 ml milk
salt and pepper
desiccated coconut
fresh fruit to garnish

recipes
eat

Coriander soup with poached egg *(açorda à Alentejana)*

Crush the garlic cloves with the salt using a pestle and mortar. Add the finely chopped coriander and put into the bottom of a serving bowl with the olive oil.

In the meantime, poach the eggs in the water and, when cooked, remove them. Then add the boiling water to the crushed ingredients, together with some of the bread and mix well. Tear the rest of the bread into pieces and add to the mixture. Use as much or as little bread as you wish.

Put the poached eggs on top of the soup and serve, each serving containing a poached egg.

Restaurante Regional de Sintra: their versions of Goan-style curry and coriander soup, and one of the tile murals depicting the town.

Ingredients (for 4 people)
4 eggs
2 garlic cloves
1 tbsp sea salt
4 tbsp olive oil
1.5 l boiling water
400 g day-old bread
4 tbsp coriander

This walk links the botanical gardens and Palace of Monserrate with the fascinating Capuchos Convent via the woods above Monserrate. The convent is a truly remarkable contrast to the spacious splendour and beauty of Monserrate's gardens — the two extremes separated by some pleasant woodland walking.

monserrate and capuchos WALK

Start the walk at the **car park/ bus stop** (**O**) opposite the entrance to **Monserrate Gardens** (208m). Walk past a water tank and **fountain** on your right, rising on a footpath over gnarled old tree roots. This takes you up to a **pond with water lilies** on your left. Turn left as you meet a surfaced track above the pond, passing a **concrete building** on your right (**3min**) and another pond on your left (ignore the fork to the left here).

At the next fork (**6min**) continue straight ahead (right) and a minute later go straight over a crossroads, climbing steadily. After reaching the top of this rise, ignore the first right turn and the second as well (**❶**; **10min**). Our walk used to head right downhill at this fork, but the area is now private property and fenced off. Keeping to the wide track, you come to the **Lagoa dos**

Distance: 5km/3mi; 1h15min as an out-and-back walk; 6.6km/4mi; 1h45min as a circuit on the return

Grade: easy-moderate, with some moderate uphill stretches and about 150m/490ft of ascent/descent overall for the linear route, 225m/740ft for the circuit. Always good underfoot, on forestry tracks and paths. *IGE 1:25,000 M888 Series map, sheets 415 and 416*

Equipment: see pages 14-15

Transport: 🚆 from Lisbon to Sintra (very frequent; see page 142), then 🚌 1253 from the train station to Monserrate (4km). Or 🚗 to Monserrate (38° 47.508'N, 9° 25.163'W)

Refreshments:
Only at Sintra; nothing en route

Opening times/Prices
All are closed 25/12 and 1/1; www.parquesdesintra.pt. You need a ticket to enter the park; consider buying a combination ticket with access to the palaces and castle. Concessions.
Convento dos Capuchos daily ex 25/12 and 1/1; apr-oct 09.30-20.00; nov-mar 10.00-18.00; €9;
Monserrate Palace daily ex 25/12 and 1/1; apr-oct 09.30-19.00; nov-mar 10.00-18.00; €20 (includes **gardens**)

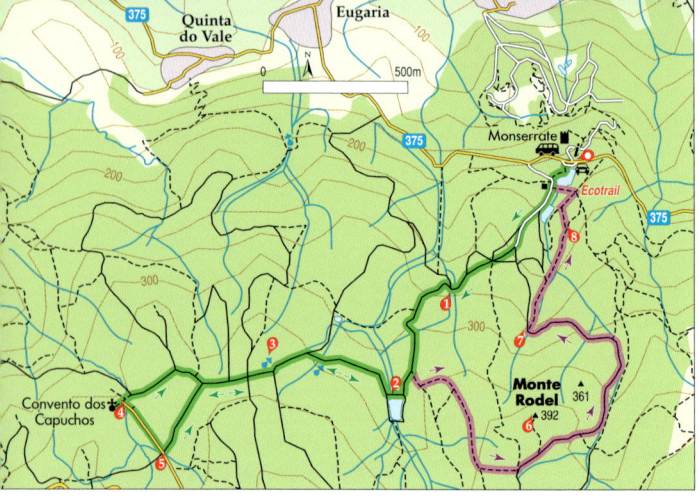

Mosqueiros (**②**;**15min**), one of the beauty spots on this walk. Further along the track, you pass a **water storage tank** (**③**) on your left (it has a small *azulejo* panel with the date 1888 on the far wall). After another 220 metres you will come to the track to the ticket office for the convent. If you already have your ticket, carry on to the fairy tale setting of the **Convento dos Capuchos** itself (**④**; **30min**), described in the panel opposite.

After your visit retrace your steps to **②**; the way divides at this lake. Decide if you will take the longer route or just retrace your steps along the track.

To take the longer route, head back the way you came for just under 100 metres, then turn right for 50 metres and, at a crossroad of tracks go left. Stay on this wide path , ignoring any side paths, for 450m, then turn left. About 200 metres along, you can take a path up to **Monte Rodel** (**⑥**), but you will need a head for heights on this granite boulder field — where you have a 360° overlook of the Sintra-Cascais Natural Park and, if conditions are right, you'll have a view over the 'sea of clouds'.

Ignore a track to the right beyond the Monte Rodel ascent and, 400 metres further on (by which time you are on a stone-laid track), fork left. After 350 metres on this new track, fork right on a path (**6**). Follow it downhill, among giant ferns, low 'walls' of a watercourse, and first a wood-carved bear hidden in the woods on the right and then two foxes. After 50 metres turn left on another path (**8**). When you come to some small ponds, you'll see a signposted 1km-long 'Ecotrail' with fingerposts and info boards that lead you gently back to the **car park/bus stop** (**O**; **1h45min**).

You can buy a ticket to visit the gardens of Monserrate at the **Visitor Centre** (**a**) across the road if you have not already bought a ticket online.

The Convento dos Capuchos was founded in 1590 and provides a stark contrast to the splendour of Monserrate.
The tiny monastery is located in the midst of a jumble of huge rocks and boulders and takes austerity to the limit. The individual cells, sufficient for a dozen inmates, are built into the rock, the only insulation provided by cork lining the doors and ceilings. Beds were simply cork bark laid out on the floor.
A guided visit is a fascinating way to learn about the layout and functionality of this hideaway — and about the harsh life and discipline of the monks.

Monserrate Park: the gardens and park have existed since the end of the 18th century, from which time various owners and tenants have attempted to create a botanical garden.

The writer William Beckford rented the property from 1794 and created, amongst other things, the waterfall just inside the entrance. However, most influential of all in the development of the park was Sir Francis Cook (1st Viscount of Monserrate), who acquired the property in 1856. Apart from extensive landscaping and planting, he engaged the English architect James Knowles, together with a thousand workers to create the neo-oriental palace (the exterior of which has fairly recently been restored).

The artist William Stockdale was also involved at the time in developing the botanical gardens. In 1949 ownership passed to the Portuguese State and, after decades of relative neglect, in the 1990s the park and buildings were the subject of extensive restoration work lasting several years.

Café de Paris

This well known restaurant is just in front of the National Palace. Sitting on the esplanade, watching the horse and carriages drive past, takes you back to the romantic era of the 19th

century. If you eat indoors, look at the lovely painted ceiling. Good service, well-presented meals, and a reasonably-priced three-course menu. Unlike some of the other 'touristy' restaurants in Sintra, the Café de Paris features some authentic Portuguese dishes.

CAFE DE PARIS
Praça a República, 32, Sintra
☏ 219 232 375; www.screstauracao.com
daily from 09.00-22.00 €€€

light meals including **sandwiches**, **salads** and **omelettes**

starters include *melão com presunto* (melon with smoked ham), soups, prawns done in various ways and the 'Chef's starter': *carapaus de escabeche* (marinated horse-mackerel; recipe on page 53).

grilled **fish** and **combination fish and seafood** dishes based on traditional recipes, like *bacalhau com broa* (cod with carn bread), *arroz de marisco* (seafood rice) and *açorda do marisco* (seafood mixed with bread, coriander and egg).

meat dishes include various steaks. We also recommend *peito de frango recheado com espinafres e nozes* (chicken breast stuffed with spinach and nuts; recipe on page 52) and the *cabrito à moda de colares* (roast kid Colares-style, with a very rich gravy).

sweets include ice-cream, fresh fruit and offers from the trolley

vegetarian and vegan menus

---

restaurants
eat

Chicken breast stuffed with spinach and nuts
(peito de frango recheado com espinafres e nozes)

Make a pocket in each of the 4 chicken breasts, season with salt, pepper and lemon juice.

Mix the nuts and chopped spinach together and stuff the chicken breasts with the mixture, then secure with skewers.

Heat the butter in a frying pan, but do not let it burn. Add the chicken breasts, turning down the heat and gently fry, turning occasionally, until cooked.

Top with the sauce and serve with plain boiled rice.

Ingredients (for 4 people)
4 chicken breasts
1 cup of lightly boiled, well drained, spinach
20 g nuts (chopped walnuts, almonds or pine nuts)
1 lemon
2 tbsp butter
salt and pepper
For the sauce
600 ml basic white sauce
1 tbsp cream
1 tsp curry powder

Chicken with spinach and nuts at the Café de Paris, with extra spinach served in a wine glass. Opposite: the restaurant's presentation of the *carapaus* and a general display

recipes

Marinated horse-mackerel (carapaus de escabeche)

Horse-mackerel are small, sardine-like fish so, if you make the recipe back home, use small sardines.

Clean and dry the *carapaus*, dip in flour, shake off surplus then fry in hot olive oil until slightly browned. Place in a glass or ceramic dish with a lid.

To prepare the marinade: Simmer all the ingredients in a covered saucepan for 15 minutes, then pour the mixture over the fish. Cover and leave to marinate for 3 days in the refrigerator. Serve cold.

Ingredients (for 4 people)
1 kg *carapaus* (or small sardines)
flour
olive oil

for the marinade
100 ml white vinegar
300 ml dry white wine
100 ml water
1 tsp salt
pepper
2 carrots, grated
2 onions, sliced
2 cloves garlic, finely chopped
1 tbsp chopped parsley
100 ml olive oil
1 bay leaf

Perched at 487m atop the westernmost summit of the Sintra Hills, Peninha Chapel provides wonderful views out to Cabo da Roca, Guincho Beach and the Cascais-Estoril coast. Legend has it that at this spot the Virgin Mary appeared as a beautiful girl before a mute shepherdess and gave her speech.

peninha circuit from azóia

WALK

peninha circuit from azóia **walk 4**

To commemorate this miracle, a humble chapel was built in thanks to the Virgin. The present chapel and surrounding buildings date back to 1753 and now have a somewhat austere and abandoned aspect. The place can get very busy at weekends, as it is possible to drive very nearly to the top. This should not detract from the walk which, although a fairly stiff climb up, keeps well away from roads and passes through some varied scenery. The main walk up is mostly through woodland, so you will do the hard work in the shade; the return downhill is on the sparsely-vegetated southwest face of the Sintra range, which provides a remarkable contrast to the luxuriant vegetation seen everywhere else in these hills.

> **Distance:** 5.9km/3.7mi; 1h20min
>
> **Grade:** easy-moderate, with an ascent/descent of 220m/720ft. Much of the walk is on good forestry tracks, although the main ascent is on a steep woodland footpath. *IGE 1:25,000 M888 Series map, sheet 415*
>
> **Equipment:** see pages 14-15
>
> **Transport:** 🚆 to Sintra as page 142, then Carris 🚌 1624 to Azoia (alight at the stop 'Estrada do Cabo da Roca'; journey time is about 35 minutes. This same service goes through to Cascais, from where you can also catch a 🚆 into Lisbon. Or 🚗 to/from Azóia (38° 46.408'N, 9° 28.729'W)
>
> **Refreshments:** restaurants and cafés in Azóia; *nothing en route*

Start the walk at the **road junction above Azóia** (where the EN247-4 to Cabo Roca leaves the main EN247; 🔴). There is a **bus shelter** here or, if you have come by car, head along the EN247-4 towards Azóia for just 60 metres, then turn right; there are places to park alongside this road — either opposite the recycling bins or further along on the right.

walk & eat LISBON

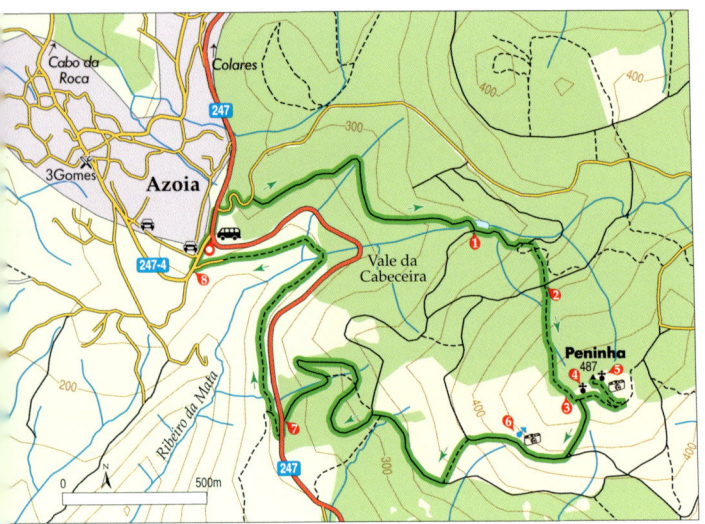

From the **bus shelter** walk 50 metres along the road (towards Colares) and then turn right up the tarred road, following the **brown signpost** to 'Convento de Peninha'. You will come to a **metal canopy** structure behind a fence on the right, on a sharp left-hand bend (**4min**). Turn right on the dirt road immediately after the fence. Continue on the level along this forestry track, passing a white SMAS **valve housing** on the left (**7min**). The track swings round to the right (**10min**), crosses a small watercourse and soon begins to rise. On another right-hand bend (**❶**; **17min**), be sure to bear left at the fork, skirting to the right of a pond. Two minutes later the track swings round to the left; on the outside of this bend, take the path leading steeply up to the right, into the pine woods.

The spreading heads of cypresses *(Cupressus lusitanica)* form a dense canopy along this path, under which little else but the carpet of ivy can grow. Cross straight over an earthen track (❷; **23min**) and follow the path up the hill ahead. You emerge at the top of the woods, by a **blocked gateway** in an old stone wall (❸; **30min**). Turn right and then go immediately left through a gap in the wall, following the footpath beyond it. You now get extensive views out over the coast and back to the mouth of the Tagus.

The path leads up below spreading cypresses, through a carpet of ground ivy

On joining a dirt track, turn left uphill. You will see some red and yellow 'SINT 10' fingerposts here, as well as some information boards. You pass a ruined chapel, the **Ermida de São**

Hazy-day view from Peninha to Cabo da Roca

Saturnino (④), and arrive at the wall below Peninha (**33min**). As you rise to approach this wall, turn sharp left, onto another track just above, now continuing just below the wall. This leads you immediately to some steps which give access to the walled-in area of the main chapel and the several buildings of the **Santuario da Peninha** (487m; ⑤; **35min**).

After taking in the fabulous views, retrace your steps down to the ruined chapel (**4**; **38min**). Turn left on the wide dirt track leading downhill just past this and, after just under 200 metres, take the right-hand fork, following another dirt track downhill. Look out along here for pale pink to white sea pinks *(Armeria pseudoarmeria)* and the shrubby pimpernel, *Anagellis moneli,* with its small clear blue flowers. Carry on round to the right where another dirt road comes in from the left and in another minute you will see Cabo da Roca in the distance.

After passing a **water pumping station** on the right (**6**; **43min**), turn left at a junction (**46min**). You pass some shrubs that look suspiciously like *Grevillea* that must have 'escaped' from one of Sintra's formal gardens. At the next major T-junction of tracks, turn right downhill, emerging at an old gateway (**52min**). Walk through, turn left and, one minute later, at another T-junction, turn left again. This dirt track takes you down to the main EN247 road (**7**; **1h04min**).

Turn left for 50 metres, then cross the road and take the lane off right, which you follow parallel to and below the main road. Continue straight ahead at a fork (**1h06min**) and, now on a concrete surface, cross a **stream** (**1h13min**), beyond which the lane rises steadily up to Azóia. When you come out on the EN247-4 (**8**), turn right; the **bus shelter and starting point** is just 120m up the road (**O**; **1h20min**).

There are several restaurants in Azóia, popular with visitors on their way to or from Cabo da Roca. This restaurant serves traditional Portuguese dishes in a homely setting.

3Gomes

In the past we were welcomed with the selection of *petiscos* shown opposite — olives, *presunto* (smoked ham), a *saloio* (cows') cheese, locally-baked bread and butter. Now there is a charge (sign of the times …).

> While we enjoyed the tubot and prawn kebab, another speciality is this perfectly creamy *risotto de lagosta* with grilled lobster

3GOMES
Estrada do Cabo da Roca, 23 Azóia
(219 290 850
facebook.com/restaurante3gomes
daily from 12.30-22.30 €€

varied menu with **omelettes** and **salads** for a light meal

vegetarian and gf dishes

charcoal-grilled fish and meat are top **specialities** … which also include *arroz de marisco* (seafood rice), *açorda do marisco* (seafood mixed with bread, coriander and egg), *polvo* (octopus), *robalo* (bass), *sargo* (sea-bream) and *linguado* (sole) freshly caught from Cabo da Roca, as well as fish and meat *espetadas* (kebabs)

seafood also features very prominently — including *lagosta* (lobster), *camarão* (prawns), *percebes* (barnacles) and *amêijoas* (cockles)

meat dishes include the mixed meat kebab, steak au poivre or 'steak a café', grilled chicken, roast kid, pork chops, escalopes of beef with mushroom in a Madeira sauce and *javali* (wild boar)…

plenty of choice for **sweets**, including fresh fruit, both local and exotic, chocolate mousse, sweet rice (recipe page 103), rum baba, ice-cream and many more

restaurants
eat

recipes • **pão de trigo**

Turbot and prawn kebab *(espetada de peixe com camarão)*

Preheat the grill to moderate while you assemble the kebabs. Cut each fillet of turbot into 6 pieces and thread onto a skewer, alternating with the red and green peppers, the onion and the prawns.

Brush the kebabs with olive oil and cook them on the grill, turning them every 2 minutes until they are cooked.

Serve with boiled potatoes, carrots, beans and broccoli (or any vegetables that are in season) and a small dish of tartar sauce.

Preparing the kebabs at home

'Petiscos' (appetizers) at 3Gomes

Ingredients (for 4 people)

- 4 thick fillets of turbot (or any other chunky, firm white fish)
- 12 squares of green pepper
- 12 squares of red pepper
- 2 large onions
- 12 raw prawns
- 2 tbsp olive oil
- 4 skewers

recipes
eat

The coast west of Colares has long attracted summer visitors from Sintra, as an alternative to Lisbon's Cascais and Estoril beaches. Indeed, so popular was this route to the sea that a 12km-long tramline *(eléctrico)* was built all the way from Sintra to Praia das Maçãs. In summer you can use this practical route to start the walk.

azenhas do mar
WALK

Start the walk at Várzea de Colares, at the junction with the EN375 road to Praia das Maçãs (**O**). Set off along the right-hand side of the road, crossing the **Ribeira de Colares** and then passing the the **Adega Cooperativa** (**1**; 1min) on the right. (The *eléctrico* stops opposite this wine co-op, so if you come by the tram, start out here.) Keep on the main road past the turn-off right to Mucifal (**4min**), but then turn right on a narrow surfaced road (Rua de Brancaflor; **6min**). After just under 300 metres, bear right at a fork on Rua da Peregrinacão (**9min**). You pass through a belt of summer homes on either side.

Ignoring all side turnings, continue straight on — first across a small **stream** (**24min**) and then across another lane (**29min**). Soon after passing a **caravan site** (**2**) on the left,

Distance: 11.5km/7.1mi; 2h11min

Grade: easy; good underfoot, with very gentle ups and downs, mostly on lanes. *IGE 1:25,000 M888 Series map, sheet 415*

Equipment: see pages 14-15

Transport: hourly Carris 🚌 1254 to 'Avenida 25 de Abril'; same bus to return); journey time abut 15 minutes. 🚌 Or you can take the tram mentioned opposite all the way to Praia das Maçãs, a journey of about 45 minutes; board it near Sintra station. For timetables see www.sintraportugaltourism.com under 'Transportation'. Or 🚗 to/from Várzea de Colares (38° 48.193'N, 9° 26.997'W)

Refreshments en route: Restaurants, bars/cafés at Várzea de Colares, Azenhas do Mar, Praia Grande, Praia das Maçãs

Sintra tram *(eléctrico)*; you can take it all the way to Praia das Maçãs

Ducks in the river at Várzea de Colares

some vineyards come into view. These have nylon netting windbreaks (instead of the traditional bamboo canes) and are not very extensive. Wine production in the Colares region is under ever-increasing pressure from property developers. Keep ahead past the vineyards, join another lane coming in from the left (**42min**) and soon come to the outskirts of Azenhas do Mar.

Turn left at the tarmac road in front of the café Adega das Azenhas (**44min**) and pass a small bandstand and then a church and chapel on the right. This takes you into the upper square of **Azenhas do Mar** (**47min**). There are shops and a couple of bars where you can have some refreshments. Then continue in the same direction towards the coast.

Fisherman perched atop the cliffs near Azenhas do Mar

When the **Escola Oficial** — a school built in the Salazar years in the 'Estado Novo' style — is on your right, turn right and then immediately left — to a **viewpoint** (**3**; **48min**) from where you can photograph the spectacular cliff scenery and the old houses of Azenhas do Mar clinging to the rockface of the headland to the north (photo on page 62).

From this *miradouro* walk back south on the main road, just to the end of the crash barrier, then turn right on a track by a red arrow on a lamppost; there may also be a 'Velocidad Controlada' sign on the road (**❹**; **50min**). From here you can walk along the cliff tops towards Praia das Maçãs for a while. The scenery is spectacular, and you will doubtless see fishermen perched on the cliff top, casting their lines into the heaving swell 40 metres below. Eventually private properties block the way along the cliff, and you are forced to rejoin the main road (**58min**). Follow the road into **Praia das Maçãs**, taking the fork down right to the **beach** (**❺**; **1h07min**).

Just by the beach-front restaurants (Loureiro and Neptune) you should see red and white waymarks and a signpost for the GR11. Walk out across the beach towards the low cliff opposite. You will need to cross the stream (**1h10min**) at its narrowest point, just in front of the headland. If there has been very heavy rain (occasionally possible in the winter) it can be *dangerous* to try crossing here.*

Climb up the lower ramp, close to the sea (alternatively, climb up a little way back from the cliff edge), to reach the **top of the headland** (**1h13min**). Then follow the sandy track along the cliff top. Keep ahead, ignoring the track down to Rodizio

---

*In this case you should *retrace your steps to the village* and then follow the main road out towards Colares. Turn right at the roundabout reached in 10 minutes by the brown sign to 'Praia Grande' and immediately cross the stream on the road. You can now either just follow the road up the hill and then down into Praia Grande (rejoining the main walk in 15 minutes), or turn right immediately after the bridge and follow the track that runs alongside the stream back out to the headland.

Traditional viniculture north of Azenhas do Mar, with cane windbreaks

Beach (**1h19min**), soon passing a café and restaurant on the left. Praia Grande comes into view ahead, and you join the tarmac road leading to it.

Walk down the road and along the front, until you come to a small roundabout in front of the Casa da Galé Restaurant (see

Walk 6, pages 82-83; **1h30min**). Continue ahead until the (heavily graffitied) **white wall** on your left ends, then follow a track uphill to the left (**6**). On coming to a crossroads (**1h33min**), turn left. Walk along the lane (Rua da Lagoa de Baixo), parallel with the shore below. You pass through a residential area, then hairpin up right to a T-junction (**1h38min**), where you turn left. This

Restaurante Casa da Galé (see pages 82-83)

lane (Rua da Lagoa) climbs steadily and swings round to the right; soon, as you crest the rise, Pena Palace appears in the distance.

When you reach a main road (EN601; **7**; **1h43min**), cross over and keep straight on at the crossroads immediately after, continuing downhill along the lane ahead. This tarmac-surfaced lane will take you down through attractive mixed pine and mimosa woods. You pass a turning left (Rua das Areias), after which the lane begins to level out. Ignore a track off right (**8**; **1h53min**), but turn right into Rua Mesquita at a crossroads a minute later (where a dirt track straight ahead, signed as a cul-de-sac) leads to a water treatment plant). Take the next left turn two minutes later (still on Rua Mesquita), to continue through an area of market gardens. Turn left on reaching the main EN247 road (**2h10min**) at **Várzea de Colares**. Walk back downhill for one minute, to the junction where the walk began (**O**).

There are a couple of good restaurants in Várzea de Colares (and even more if you are prepared to walk up the hill to Colares village itself). We came to thoroughly enjoy the Ribeirinha de Colares — for all the right reasons: good food, a pleasant, 'warm' ambience, and very helpful staff.

Ribeirinha de Colares

This restaurant specialises in meals that reflect traditional Portuguese flavours. The menu, which varies daily to offer the very freshest of ingredients at the best value for money, is very tempting, and it is always difficult to choose between the imaginative dishes on offer.

There is also a delicatessen and grocery shop where you can find Portuguese cheeses, pâtés, smoked ham and other Portuguese and foreign products. Some of the finest Portuguese wines, including, of course, a selection of the famous Colares

Dining room at Ribeirinha de Colares

restaurants • várzea de colares and azenhas do mar

> **RESTAURANTE VÁRZEA**
> Largo Infante D. Henriques, 6
> Várzea de Colares (219 292 169
> daily from 09.00-24.00
> €-€€
>
> wide selection of excellent **pizzas** and **salads** for a light meal
>
> **main courses** include grilled **steak**, **fish** and **chicken** dishes

> **RIBEIRINHA DE COLARES**
> Av Bombeiros Voluntários, 71
> Várzea de Colares (219 282 175
> www.ribeirinhadecolares.com
> daily except Mondays from 12.30-14.30 and 19.30-21.45 €€
>
> wide range of **traditional meals**
>
> **entradas** include olives, local cheese and pão caseiro (freshly baked country-style bread), served with flor do olival (a very fine olive oil, in which you dip the bread)

reds, are to be found in the wine section.

Another good restaurant in Várzea de Colares, less sophisticated, but with wholesome food and a friendly atmosphere is just over the road from Ribeirinha de Colares, alongside the bridge: the **Restaurante da Várzea**. You can enjoy your meal here sitting on the esplanade. In summer there is live music. (But it was temporarily closed at press date.)

The spectacularly located **Restaurante Azenhas do Mar**, clinging to th cliffs alongside the swimming pool at Azenhas do Mar (with a lovely patio), is another good option — and very popular; reserve ahead!

> **AZENHAS DO MAR**
> Piscinas das Azenhas do Mar
> Tel: 219 280 739
> www.azenhasdomar.com
> daily except Mondays from 12.00-22.30 €€
>
> **specialises in charcoal-grilled fresh fish and seafood** (the price of the fish depends on the weight, so always ask the price before ordering — or you may have a bit of a shock!)
>
> other **seafood** offerings include caril de gambas (prawn curry; recipe page 44) and polvo assado (roast octopus)
>
> **meat** dishes include pork, roast beef and duck.
>
> delicious **desserts** — like passion fruit mousse — and 'desserts of the day'

Rabbit stew (ensopado de coelho à Alentejano)

Fry the chopped onions, crushed garlic and rabbit portions all together in the olive oil until the rabbit has turned brown. Then add the stock, red wine and bay leaf. Season with salt and pepper.

Bring to the boil and cook gently for about 3-4 minutes, then add the quartered potatoes. Bring to the boil again. Cover and simmer until the rabbit and potatoes are cooked (about 20-30 minutes.

Ingredients (for 4 people)
- 1 rabbit, jointed
- 2 onions, finely chopped
- 2 garlic cloves, crushed
- 2 tbsp olive oil
- 200 ml stock
- 300 ml red wine (preferably the local Colares)
- 0.5 kg potatoes
- 1 bay leaf
- salt and pepper
- chopped parsley, to garnish
- 4 thick slices of fried *pão caseiro* (or a dense, day-old bread)

Place the fried bread in 4 deep serving dishes and cover with rabbit portions. Spoon the potatoes around the bread and rabbit and pour the juice over. Garnish with chopped parsley.

This dish (shown here as served at the Ribeirinha de Colares restaurant) is a cross between a soup and a stew. The *pão caseiro* they use is baked locally.

recipes

eat

ribeirinha de colares

Prawn bread soup
(açorda de camarão)

Like the rabbit dish opposite, this is a cross between a soup and a stew. Cook the prawns in salted boiling water for 2 minutes. Drain and keep the water. Cool the prawns, shell them and remove the heads. Return the heads and shells to the cooking water and boil uncovered for about 10 minutes, or until the liquid has reduced a little.

Pour 600 ml of this liquid over the bread, reserving the rest of the liquid — or use pre-prepared fish stock from a stock cube.

Fry the chopped garlic in the olive oil, then add the soaked bread, stirring until you have a soft, mushy consistency. Season with salt, pepper and a dash of piri-piri. Add the prawns and the finely chopped coriander and heat through.

If the soup is too dry, add some of the reserved cooking water. Finally, add the well-beaten eggs and cook, stirring gently, for 2 to 3 minutes. Check seasoning before serving.

Ingredients (for 4 people)
1 kg prawns
500 g day-old bread
3 cloves of garlic
4 eggs, well beaten
4 tbsp olive oil
600 ml stock (fish stock cube or water in which the prawns have been cooked; a glass of white wine could be included in the total liquid)
4 tbsp fresh coriander
salt and pepper
piri-piri (see page 110)

Cabo da Roca, the westernmost point of mainland Europe, is the final goal of this walk, and you can even get a certificate to prove you've been there! But even if you don't go the whole way, you will see some wonderfully dramatic coastal scenery, bird life and wild flowers — all with bracing sea air and the roar of the ocean!

westward to cabo da roca
WALK

westward to cabo da roca **walk 6**

Start the walk at **Praia das Maçãs** (**O**). Just by the beachfront restaurants (Loureiro and Neptune) you will see red and white waymarks and a signpost for the GR11. Walk out across the beach towards the low cliff opposite. You will need to cross the stream (**3min**) at its narrowest point, just in front of the headland. If there has been very heavy rain (occasionally possible in the winter) it can be *dangerous* to try crossing here. Should this be the case, refer to the footnote on page 67.

Climb up the lower ramp, close to the sea (alternatively, climb up a little way back from the cliff edge), to reach the **top of the headland** (**6min**). A sandy track leads you along the cliff top, where the invasive Hottentott fig, *Caprobutus edulis*, with its succulent leaves and large yellow flowers, is much in

Distance: 11km/6.8mi; 2h52min (one way)

Grade: moderate. There are some steep gradients from the beaches up onto the cliff tops and an ascent of 80m/265ft near the end of the walk; otherwise the walk is fairly easy going. Most of the route is waymarked (red/white for the GR11, yellow/red for the PR7). *IGE 1:25,000 M888 Series map, sheet 415*

Equipment: see pages 14-15

Transport: Carris 🚌 1248 from Sintra to Praia das Maçãs; alight at the 'Praia' stop (journey time about 25 minutes). Or take the 🚋 from Sintra (see pages 62-63). Return from Cabo da Roca bus station on Carris 🚌 1253 — either back to Sintra station (journey time 45 minutes) or 🚌 1624 to Cascais (30 minutes), from where you can catch a 🚆 to Lisbon.

Shorter version: 🚗 If you have your own transport, you could do an out-and-back walk along the cliff tops from Praia Grande (38° 48.792'N, 9° 28.655'W)

Refreshments en route: Bars, cafés and restaurants at Praia das Maçãs, Praia Grande, Praia da Adraga, Cabo da Roca and nearby Azóia (see page 60)

Praia Grande, from the trig point reached in 40min

evidence. Keep ahead, ignoring the track down to Rodizio Beach (**12min**), soon passing a café and restaurant on the left. Praia Grande comes into view ahead, and you join the tarmac road leading to it (**15min**). Walk down the road and along the front until you come to a small roundabout in front of the Casa da Galé Restaurant (**23min**; see page 82). Even if you're not ready for lunch, do take a break here.

Then continue ahead, down the ramp and onto the sand. At first there seems to be no continuation off the beach, but in just a couple of minutes you will see the handrails of a long stairway up to the cliff top. Climb the steps — all 320 of them —and, once at the top (**34min**), turn right, following the waymarks out to a **viewpoint** (❶; **40min**). You will certainly want to pause here, to

Pistacia lentiscus (top) and the old lime kiln at Praia da Adraga

recuperate from the climb and take in the particularly fine view to the north over the great expanse of Praia Grande shown on page 77.

Heading on from here, navigation is very easy, as you are following both the GR11 and the PR7. The red and white and yellow and white waymarks guide you across the cliff top towards Praia da Adraga. The joints in the limestone surface have weathered here to a karst pavement, where the larger cracks and fissures are filled with wind-blown sand or in some cases provide shelter for vegetation and flowers such as sweet alison (*Lobularia maritima*).

Make sure you take the waymarked left turn as you approach Praia da Adraga (**49min**). (The lesser path ahead, marked with an 'X', leads to a dangerous descent to the beach.) The path now heads a short way inland, passing clumps of juniper *(Juniperus Phoenicia)*, mastic *(Pistacia lentiscus)* and, in spring, colourful *Antirrhinum major*, before dropping down through mixed woodlands of mimosa, giant reeds, pines and eucalyptus and becoming sandy underfoot. The path turns down right and soon joins a **major sandy trail** (❷; **54min**). Turn right here and walk into a stand of umbrella pines a minute later.

Walk down through these lovely trees and, when the path divides just below the trees, follow the waymarking down the right-hand fork, to reach the road (**1h01min**), passing the café, restaurant and toilets at **Praia da Adraga**. Turn left along the road, away from Praia da Adraga and, a minute later, take the **waymarked track** off right (❸; with a signpost 'Cabo da Roca 4.5km'). As the track takes you up a small valley, make sure you follow the waymarking sharply to the right (**1h07min**), then continue until you come to a T-junction at the **top of the valley** (**1h11min**).

At the T-junction the waymarking indicates that you will continue to the left, towards Cabo da Roca. However, rather than go directly there, it is well worth taking the *right turn* here and walking out to the cliffs. So turn right, and in two minutes you will come to another T-junction near the cliff top. Turn right again here and walk north for four minutes, to reach some impressive **caves and a blowhole** in the cliffs (❹; **1h16min**).

Retrace your steps to the cliff top T-junction (**1h21min**) and carry straight on along the cliffs, now heading south. The track crosses a fairly sharp little gully (**1h25min**) and rises onto the cliff top above **Praia da Ursa** (❺; **1h35min**), with views on over to Cabo da Roca. Look out for kestrels *(Falco tinnunculus)* and Peregrine falcons *(Falco peregrinus)* too.

To your right and in front of the small beach is the islet-pinnacle called Pedra da Ursa (Bear Rock). Legend has it that

Pedra de Alvidrar, seen from the point above Praia da Ursa

this (female) bear defied the instructions of the gods to move north when the Sintra ice cap started to melt. As a punishment she was turned into stone, together with her cubs, which form the lesser rocks off the shore — including Pedra de Alvidrar shown here.

The scenery is magnificent. It is tempting to try to reach the cape by carrying on straight ahead, *but do not try!* There is no proper path, and it is very steep and slippery. Instead, you could follow the GR11 which (at time of writing) carried on from here and stayed inland of the cliffs) or follow us: retrace your steps to the cliff top T-junction and turn right, back to the valley-top T-junction (**❻**; **1h52min**). From here you have the choice of turning left and retracing your steps to Praia das Maçãs (3h03min), or turning right with the PR7 and carrying on to Cabo da Roca (2h52min).

To make for Cabo da Roca, turn right and follow the track as it winds inland (thereby avoiding the deep valley of the Ursa stream). Not far past a **ruined building** on the right (**1h55min**), you will see a small area of **traditional viniculture** on the left. The track reaches its highest point (124m; **1h58min**), then starts to drop quite steeply. It takes you to a junction, where you turn right (**7**; **2h08min**), as indicated by a waymarked rock on the right. Four minutes later, as the track is rising up a small slope, it divides, but both forks rejoin at the top, where you come to a T-junction (**8**; **1h13min**). Follow the right-hand track, the PR7 signposted to Cabo da Roca.

Cross the **Ribeira da Ursa** (**2h16min**) and take the left fork just over 100 metres beyond it. Then fork right almost immediately. Another track joins from the left, and you curve around to the right, to a tarmac road (**2h29min**). Turn right here and follow the road out to **Cabo da Roca** (**9**; **2h52min**). The cape itself, at 9°30′ west of Greenwich, is the westernmost extremity of mainland Europe. A monument with a plaque explains this and quotes Luís Camões, Portugal's great poet: 'Here … where the land ends and the sea begins …' — a fitting reminder of the crucial role played by the Portuguese in discovering and opening up the trade routes of the world some 500 years ago.

Just inland from the monument there is a bar, restaurant and toilets. There is also a **tourist information office**, where you can obtain a certificate confirming your visit to the far west of Europe. From here you can either catch a bus to Cascais (then train to Lisbon), or retrace your steps to Praia das Maçãs — a very long trek, taking between 8-10 hours!

Casa da Galé/Restaurante da Adraga

Casa da Galé, shown on page 69, overlooks the huge expanse of beautiful Praia Grande and is just the place to relax — preferably on the patio — and enjoy a good meal with a glass or two of wine. The interior is decorated with ship's artefacts relating to losses at sea. There is a reasonably priced tourist menu. Or try the *highly praised*, small and rustic **Restaurante da Adraga**, nestled into the cliffs with unrestricted sea views.

The **Restaurante Cabo da Roca**, behind the souvenir shop (and temporarily closed at press date) wins no prizes for its cuisine, but its setting, perched on the cliffs above the Atlantic at Continental Europe's most westerly point — with the Serra da Sintra as a backdrop — is where everyone wants to be!

> **CASA DA GALÉ**
> Praia Grande ℂ 219 291 218
> daily from 12.00 (from 10.00 on Wednesdays)-22.00 €€
>
> **fish** (grilled, boiled or oven-baked) and **seafood**, *both sold by weight* — so always confirm the weight before ordering, otherwise it can become surprisingly expensive.
>
> **meat** dishes include the typical Portuguese **Carne de Porco à Alentejana** (pork and clams done in the regional way; recipe opposite).

> **RESTAURANTE DA ADRAGA**
> Praia da Adraga ℂ 219 280 028
> daily except Tuesdays from 12.30-21.30 (16.00 on Mondays) €€
>
> specialises primarily in **local fresh fish** either grilled or in other dishes like *caldeirada* (a fish stew); also *percebes* (barnacles), *sapateira* (crab), *lavagante* (lobster) and *lagosta* (crayfish) — all priced by weight
>
> good **local wine** from Azenhas do Mar

> **RESTAURANTE SNACK-BAR CABO DA ROCA**
> Cabo da Roca ℂ not available
> daily €-€€
>
> **light snacks and meals**: various sandwiches, *tosta mista* (toasted cheese and ham), *prego no pão* (steak roll), *bifana* (pork roll), hamburgers, omelettes, salads, fish & chips, chicken

restaurants

eat

Pork with clams, Alentejo-style
(carne de porco à Alentejana)

Cut the pork into bite-sized pieces and put into a ceramic or glass bowl. Using a pestle and mortar, crush the garlic cloves and the salt to make a paste. Rub this paste into the cubes of pork. Cover and leave in the refrigerator for 24 hours, turning the pork cubes occasionally.

Pork with clams Alentejo-style, as served at the Casa da Galé

In the meantime wash and scrub the cockles well. It is a good idea to leave them soaking in salted water for at least 2 hours. Discard any that have opened.

After the pork has marinated, fry the cubes in the hot fat and, when the pork is almost cooked, add the cockles and the wine. Cover and cook for a further 6-8 minutes, or until the cockles have opened their shells. Discard any that haven't opened.

Sprinkle with the chopped coriander to serve. Traditionally this dish is served with boiled potatoes but chips and salad are just as good. (In the photograph, the dish has been served with home-made crinkled chips.)

Ingredients (for 4 people)
800 g loin of pork
4 garlic cloves
100 g *massa de pimentão**
150 g lard
1 kg cockles
200 ml dry white wine
2 tbsp chopped coriander
salt

massa de pimentão (red pepper paste) is available in most Portuguese supermarkets. If unavailable, crush 1 garlic clove with a tsp of salt using a pestle and mortar, add 1 tbsp of sweet paprika and 1 tbsp of oil, mixing well.

The sandy, often barren countryside south of Lisbon is abruptly broken by the limestone hills on the southern side of the Arrábida Peninsula, giving rise to some quite dramatic coastal scenery between Setúbal and Cabo Espichel in the west. The area has now been designated a Natural Park.

arrábida peninsula

WALK

The objective of the Arrábida Natural Park is to protect the landscape, vegetation and wildlife from the inevitable pressures that exist due to its proximity to Lisbon. There is much to see in this relatively small area and, if you have time to explore, it is well worth visiting the park office in Setúbal; we find the staff there consistently helpful and interested. The walk we describe here is one that the Park Authority laid out some years ago, although it is no longer waymarked. In the meantime other routes have become popular, chief among them the *vigia* on the summit of São Luís, which we highlight in violet on our map.

Our timings start at the **Capela São Luís da Serra** (197m; **O**). Take the dirt road/ track that heads west from the chapel; it's initially level and passes through fine umbrella

Distance: 7.4km/4.6mi; 1h50min *(from the Capela São Luís)*; travelling by bus, you will need to add 1.4km (25min) to the overall distance/times

Grade: easy-moderate. Fairly stiff initial ascent of 100m/330ft, then most of the walk is easy underfoot and mainly level, but there are one or two short, steep sections. *IGE 1:25,000 M888 Series map, sheet 454*

Equipment: see pages 14-15

Transport: from Lisbon take Carris 🚌 4752 via Ponte 25 de Abril or 🚌 4720 via Ponte Vasco da Gama to Setúbal bus station. Both are express services departing at least hourly and taking about 1h. Change to Carris 🚌 3642 (Sesimbra bus) and alight at the São Luís Serra bus stop (journey time 10min). Mon-Fri morning departures at 08.25, 09.25, 10.25, 11.45; Sat/Sun 08.20, 10.20. Afternoon returns depart Sesimbra Mon-Fri at 14.15, 15.40, 16.45; Sat/Sun at 14.40, 16.50. Buses pass the São Luís Serra stop about 35min after Sesimbra. Or by 🚗 to/from the chapel (38° 31.762'N, 8° 55.972'W).

Refreshments:
Bars, cafés and restaurants in nearby Setúbal, none en route

walk & eat LISBON

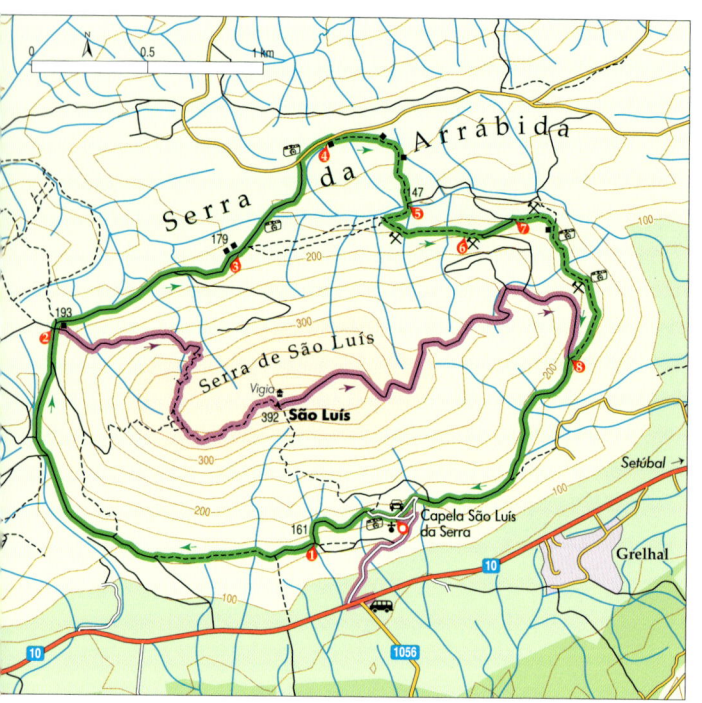

pines, with views down to the coast and Tróia beyond. Then the track starts dropping quite steeply (**4min**) until reaching a T-junction at 161m altitude (**1**; **12min**). Turn right here, passing clumps of kermes oak *(Quercus coccifera)* and mastic trees *(Pistacia lentiscus)*. The track narrows to a trail (**15min**) running through a mix of pine and olive trees.

When you drop down to join a dirt road coming in from

behind and below on the left (**21min**), follow it to the right. You pass a large **water tank** on the left by an entrance with **green gates** (**30min**) and keep on ahead on the dirt road as it climbs gently, ignoring another dirt road off to the left after just a minute. The road climbs steadily up into more open, cultivated countryside until you reach the **top of the rise** (❷; 193m; **36min**) at a crossroads with an old **concrete building** on the right. At this point you *may* see a fingerpost directing you to the *Vigia* (fire-watch station) at the summit of São Luís and decide to take that route instead; we've not done it but know it to be viable. Just don't try to take the path down from the summit direct to the chapel unless you have walking poles: it's very steep and slippery, with loose stones underfoot.

Our walk keeps straight on here, descending immediately. You pass a couple of houses on the left, after which the road starts to rise gently again. This rise takes you up to some **farm buildings** on the left (179m; ❸; **47min**).

There are soon views out ahead to the great expanse of flat country beyond the Sado Estuary (visited on Walk 8). The dirt road drops down slightly through olive groves before rising up again and meeting a tarred road (**55min**), where you turn right. Now you have some fine views over to the next ridge to the north, the Serra do Louro, where you'll spot some old windmills.

After following the tarred road for about 100m, you reach an **old ruin** on the right (❹; **57min**); turn right off the road here, on a fairly rough path which initially runs parallel to and below the tarred road. You pass in front of **another ruin** (**59min**), this

View from one of the quarries en route

one on the left. You descend into a shallow valley. Soon the path drops down and round to the right of another **ruin** (**1h04min**). The path is now a cart track and drops even further, to a small **concrete bridge** over the watercourse in the bottom of the valley (147m; ❺; **1h07min**).

Cross the bridge and follow the cart track up to the right. Almost immediately, the track turns back on itself in a hairpin bend, gains height and then levels off at an **old quarry** (❻; **1h10min**). Pleasant views open out to the hills opposite. Follow the trail past the quarry and on up to the **next abandoned quarry** (**1h14min**), now with the views out over the Sado Estuary beginning to open out. *Take care* here to follow the old road on the left downhill and out of the quarry; initially the surface is dirt, but becomes broken-up tar after just 20 metres.

As the road descends, prepare to leave it at the first **hairpin bend to the left** (❼): follow a dirt track straight ahead through a **third old quarry** (**1h19min**). The quarries on the Serra de São Luís were well known for centries — not only for their limestone but for dinosaur footprints. They only closed in the 1970s when the area became a natural park.

Continue round the hillside, with ever more extensive views out across Setúbal opening up. The trail narrows to a path at the far end of the quarry working (ignore the path down to the left here). This path now wends a delightful way around the hillside through a mix of Mediterranean oak, olive, eucalyptus and thyme until you **cross a major dirt road** (**8**) and continue along a cart track. As the track contours round the hillside, you might want to take home some wild rosemary from the bushes growing here in profusion.

Entrance to the Castelo São Felipe in Setúbal

Soon (**1h40min**) you may see some beehives just to the left; immediately afterwards, you join another cart track coming in from the left. Keep ahead; shortly the red roof and white walls of the chapel come into view. The fence you have been following on the left ends at a junction of several tracks; keep ahead on the main track which immediately joins the dirt road (**1h47min**), where you turn up right to the **São Luís Chapel** (**O**; **1h50min**).

Restaurante Bombordo

Far from the fanciest restaurant in Setúbal, Bombordo, just behind the waterfront (and opposite the unwelcoming walls of a skating rink), is certainly one of the most authentic, frequented by the locals. The restaurant serves only fish. It is famous for its *rodizio de peixe,* cooked on a huge barbecue. Each type of freshly-caught fish is grilled separately and served in recurring sequence.

Rodizio de peixe and (opposite) orange roll, as served at Bombordo

RESTAURANTE BOMBORDO
Rua do Clube Naval, 22
Setúbal (914 309 614
daily ex Mondays €-€€
credit cards are not accepted

the **speciality** is *rodizio de peixe*: *sardinhas* (sardines), *rodovalho* (halibut), *salmão* (salmon), *peixe espada* (swordfish), *cherne* (turbot), *chocos* (squid), *salmonetes* (red mullet) or whatever is in season — it just keeps coming and coming.

Served with potatoes boiled in their skins and a fresh green salad. *Azeitonas* (olives), country-style bread, and a carafe of local wine accompany this marathon. Or you could try the delicious white wine *sangria*

To finish choose from fruit in season or *doce de laranja* (orange roll; recipe opposite) — perhaps with a glass of the local Moscatel (a sweet fortified wine from Setúbal).

restaurants
eat

Rodizio de peixe

Why not try your own? For 4 people buy approximately 2.5 kg of a variety of fish such as those listed on the Bombordo menu — or any that you would like to try. The fishmonger will clean them for you if you ask, but sardines are normally left whole for grilling.

Wash the fish in cold water and dry. Sprinkle with sea salt and leave covered in the refrigerator for a few hours. When grilling, make sure the grill is hot (the coals should be white) before adding the fish. Grill each type of fish independently and serve, then grill the next type and so on.

Serve with jacket potatoes, a fresh green salad, plenty of slices of lemon, and local wine.

Orange roll *(doce de laranja* or *torta de laranja de Setúbal)*

Whisk the eggs and sugar together. Dissolve the cornflour in the orange juice and add the grated orange rind. Add the mixture to the eggs and sugar; mix well.

Grease a Swiss-roll baking tray (20.5 x 30.5 cm) with butter and line the tray with baking paper. Grease the lining paper and sprinkle with sugar. Pour the mixture into the baking tray and bake (160°C) for about 25min, until firm and golden.

Turn out onto a tea towel well sprinkled with sugar. Trim off any crisp edges and carefully roll up with the help of the tea towel. When cold, place on a serving dish and sprinkle with sugar. The roll will create its own sauce when left for a while.

Ingredients (for 4-6 people)
150 ml pure orange juice
5 large eggs
1 rounded tbsp cornflour
200 g caster sugar
grated rind of 1 orange

This walk takes you into the heart of a rice-producing area. The terrain is flat and may seem uninteresting initially, but you will encounter a wealth of flowers and bird life. Above all you will experience a unique feeling of isolation — strangely accentuated by the proximity of Setúbal's heavy industry on the far side of the estuary.

sado's rice paddies
WALK

sado's rice paddies walk 8

During the winter months the rice fields by the Sado Estuary lie fallow, and since this period coincides with major bird migrations, this can often be the best time to see the bird life — which on this walk is exceptional.

Indeed, it could be argued that after half an hour of walking through rice fields you will have had enough, but even a walker with only a modest interest in ornithology cannot fail to be impressed with the fauna on display. Depending on the time of year you are likely to see grey heron *(Ardea cinerea)*, purple heron *(Ardea purpurea)*, white storks *(Ciconia ciconia)*, little egrets *(Egretta garzetta)*, avocets *(Recurvirostra avosetta)*, marsh harriers *(Circus aeruginosus)*, black kites *(Milvus migrans)* and many others. So … plenty to keep you going a little further!

Distance: 14km/8.7mi; 3h05min (a linear walk, which can be shortened by returning at any point)

Grade: easy, level walking, but there is **no shade**. IGE 1:25,000 M888 Series map, sheets 466, 475

Equipment: see pages 14-15; take *plenty of water*, sunhats and clothing to protect from sun- and wind-burn.

Transport: 🚌 from Lisbon to Setúbal: see page 85. At Setúbal bus station check bus times from Tróia to Comporta and back (vary according to the season and ferry timetables) For ferry sailings (look for dolphins as you cross!) see www.atlanticferries.pt. From the bus station weave your way due south to Cais 3 (quay) for the catamaran to Tróia (crossing 15min; €9.10 return). On the far side either take the connecting bus (the bus stop is 50 metres up the road from the ferry) or a taxi to Comporta (20min). Or 🚗 to the Doca do Comércio in Setúbal for the car ferry to the Tróia Peninsula (it docks 3km south of Tróia; crossing 25min; car plus driver €20.40/€36.70 return; extra passengers €5.40 each). Park in Comporta (38° 22.919'N, 8° 47.315'W).

Refreshments:
cafés, bars and restaurants in Setúbal and Comporta; none en route

walk & eat LISBON

Just before you come into Comporta, you pass the sign for Restaurante Ilha do Arroz; this is where we currently suggest you eat. Shortly after, as you enter the village, you come to the Museu do Arroz (Rice Museum) on the right. The bus stop is just beyond it; if you are in a taxi, get the driver to drop you off

sado's rice paddies **walk 8**

Bank in Comporta, with the obligatory stork's nest

walk & eat LISBON

sado's rice paddies **walk 8**

Opposite: grey heron; above: typical barn made with reeds and planking, near Comporta

here. Walk along the main road towards the village and, 80 metres beyond the restaurant, turn down left off the main road and walk between the old blue and white town gateposts. Just after these, turn left on a dirt road, passing a notice board for the Sado Estuary Natural Park and a small parking area (if you have come by car, park here). *Walk timings are from this point.*

Start out at the **natural park notice board** (⭕): walk along the dirt road immediately ahead of you, keeping the tall **cane hedges** on your right. You immediately see the first **rice fields** off to the left and will start to pass small sheds containing pumps for irrigating the rice. At a fork (**9min**) keep straight ahead, still on a dirt road, but now less used and with grass down the centre. At a crossroads (**14min**), keep straight on — noticing (depending on the time of year) the small vegetable patches on the right, often with seaweed compost spread over the sandy soil.

Before long you come to a small group of houses and sheds (**Cambado;** ❶; **21min**). Keep straight on between them and, at the far end, turn left at the T-junction. Immediately afterwards, where the dirt road divides, bear right and keep straight on until you cross the **main irrigation channel** (❷; **30min**). Immediately after crossing this, turn left on a well-used dirt road which runs parallel to the irrigation channel.

Eventually you reach a junction, with an **iron grid** and **small concrete building** on the right and a **concrete valve housing** on the left (❸; **48min**). Over to the left, 20 metres away, is a **water channel**. It is worth taking a look here for waders, including avocets. There are various tracks leading off from the opposite side of the main dirt road, and following these can be quite rewarding for bird-spotters.

From this junction just keep heading straight on (northwest), eventually passing some old buildings off to the left at **Matutro** (❹). Still continuing ahead, the main dirt road bends to the right and you come to a **T-junction** (❺; **1h38min**). Just beyond is the Sado River estuary, with views over to Setúbal and its heavy industry.

From here retrace your steps to the **natural park noticeboard** and small **car park** (⭕; **3h05min**). Take some time to visit the museum, even if you're not having a meal there.

sado's rice paddies **walk 8**

While rice features extensively in Portuguese cooking, you may not realise that Portugal is quite a significant producer; in 2022 the country produced just short of 160,000 tonnes.

The average per capita annual consumption of rice in Portugal is 16 kg; this is the highest level in the European Union and totals some 300,000 tonnes per annum. About half the rice consumed is grown within Portugal, and about 45% of that production comes from the Alentejo (the rest from Ribatejo, Beira Litoral and Estremadura).

The flat rice paddies are ploughed using cage-wheeled tractors and then irrigated ready for sowing in May. About three weeks later the water is drained to encourage root development. Irrigation then continues until one or two weeks ahead of harvest (late October, when the water is drained off). Normally about 6 tonnes of rice are produced per hectare.

The huge expanse of rice fields near Comporta is a haven for bird life, especially in winter, when the fields lie fallow and birds are migrating.

Museu do Arroz and Ilha do Arroz

The museum used to house a fascinating restaurant but sadly this is currently closed (the museum can still be visited, see details at the right). We well recall eating some really tasty and imaginative dishes here, surrounded by pictures of the old rice factory and with with some bizarre flying herons as decor. The menu used to provide an appropriate emphasis on rice dishes and, in recognition of this, we are continuing to feature the razor-shell and cockle rice recipe that we so enjoyed (see page 102).

We hope the Museum's retaurant will reopen, but in the meantime we suggest the **Ilha do Arroz** which is under the same ownership as the Museu do Arroz and situated on the beach at Comporta, about 200 yards from the main road. This restaurant/bar is just the place to while away an afternoon,

Beach by the Restaurante Ilha do Arroz; right: rice ball served as a *petisco*

restaurants

eat

restaurants • **museu de arroz & ilha do arroz**

ILHA DO ARROZ
Praia da Comporta
(265 490 510
daily ex Tue from 10.00-23.00)
€€-€€€
Multibanco debit cards only

good choice of **salads, soup** and **petiscos** (little snacks) — including *gambas à guilho* (prawns in garlic), *ovos mexidos com farinheira* (scrambled eggs with sausages), and *amêijoas à Bulhão Pato* (cockles Bulhão Pato-style; recipe page 105).

rice also features here, with *arroz de tamboril* (monkfish rice), *arroz de polvo* (octopus rice), *arroz do mar* (seafood rice) and *arroz de pato* (duck rice; recipe on page 104)

steaks and **fried fish**, both served with tomato rice

vegetarian and **vegan** options

At the Museu do Arroz

especially after enjoying a snack or lunch washed down with a jug of *sangria*). Neither the museum nor the restaurant has a website at present, but the Comporta website www.herdadedacomporta.pt covers both (and others).

MUSEU DO ARROZ
EN253-1, Comporta
(965 280 465

Whilst the resturant is closed, the museum can be visited and is open from Tuesdays to Sundays from 10.00-19.00 (closed 13.00-14.00 for lunch) during July to September. Entry 7.50€. Between October and June visits are by appointment only; see the website www.herdadeda comporta.pt. There is an *adega* (wine callar) next to the museum selling excellent wines.

WAYS WITH RICE — MUSEU DO ARROZ

Razor-shell and cockle rice (arroz de langueirão)

Clean the *langueirões* and cockles in salted water to remove any particles of sand. When cleaned put the *langueirões* and cockles in a saucepan of salted water over a high heat until they open.

Remove the *langueirões* from their shells, but leave the cockles in their shells (after discarding any that haven't opened). Put the cockles to one side and reserve the water.

Chop the onion, pepper and garlic and fry in the olive oil. When the onion is opaque, add the chopped coriander or parsley and the reserved water. The water will need to be about 3 times the volume of the rice; add more water if necessary. Add the washed rice and *langueirões*.

Cook gently until the rice is soft — the mixture should not be too dry. Just before serving add the cooked cockles and stir together.

Ingredients (for 4 people)
12 *langueirões* (razor-shell clams)
24 cockles
300 g rice (the restaurant uses local 'arroz carolino', which can be bought at the nearby Atlantic Rice Company)
4 tbsp olive oil
1 large onion
1 green or red pepper or a mixture of both
1 garlic clove
coriander or parsley, chopped
salt

Sweet rice pudding *(arroz doce)*

Wash the rice, then add to a saucepan of salted boiling water. Bring to the boil and cook the rice for 2 minutes. In another saucepan boil the milk with the lemon peel and cinnamon stick.

Drain the rice and rinse under cold water. Add to the boiling milk, bring milk to the boil again, stir and leave to cook, uncovered, on a low heat for about 30 minutes, or until the milk has been absorbed and the rice is soft.

Remove from the heat, take out the pieces of lemon rind and cinnamon stick. Then quickly stir in the sugar, beaten egg yolks and butter. Return the rice to a very low heat and cook slowly for a few minutes, *without boiling*, to cook the egg yolks.

Pour the mixture into individual shallow dishes or one large shallow dish, to a thickness of about 2 cm. Decorate with cinnamon and chill for 1-2 hours.

Ingredients (for 4 people)
125 g short-grain rice
120 g caster sugar
750 ml milk
3 egg yolks
40 g butter
1 tsp salt
3-4 strips of lemon peel
1 cinnamon stick and ground cinnamon

WAYS WITH RICE — ILHA DO ARROZ

Duck rice (*arroz de pato*)

Cook the duck, remove the skin and shred the flesh. Reserve the cooking water. Cook the rice in plenty of boiling salted water.

When the rice is cooked, strain and pour boiling water over it, then drain. Add the shredded pieces of duck, the currants and the pine nuts. If the mixture is too dry, add some of the reserved cooking water.

Season with salt and a dash of *piri-piri*. Put the mixture into a shallow oven-proof dish, garnish with the slices of *chouriço* and cook in a moderate oven for 15-20 minutes.

Ingredients (for 4 people)
1 duck (2.5 kg)
300 g long-grain rice
1 *chouriço* sausage (spicy sausage)
40 g pine nuts
40 g currants
salt
piri-piri (see page 142)

Left and opposite: the recipes as served at Ilha do Arroz. Previous pages: razor-shell and cockle rice at the Museu do Arroz and sweet rice pudding made at home

recipes
eat

Cockles Bulhão Pato-style
(*amêijoas à Bulhão Pato*)

This dish originates from Lisbon and is associated with the Portuguese Romantic poet, Raimundo Bulhão Pato (1837-1912), who had creative gastronomic skills. Although he lived mostly just south of Lisbon, he spent time in Sintra and Colares with other well-known literary figures of the day.

Wash and scrub clean the cockles in salted water, changing the water several times (or leave them to soak for 2 hours before using).

Heat the olive oil and fry the chopped garlic cloves until they are beginning to colour. Add the cockles and the finely chopped coriander and season with salt and pepper.

Fry gently, shaking the pan occasionally, until the cockles have opened. Discard any that have not opened. Sprinkle with lemon juice and serve with slices of lemon.

Ingredients (for 4 people)
1 kg cockles (*amêijoas*)
2 tbsp olive oil
2 garlic cloves
1 lemon
1 bunch of coriander
salt and pepper

Cabo Espichel is perhaps best visited out of season; on a partly cloudy day you can experience the wildness of the setting — an 'end of the world' feeling, with waves crashing on the rocks over 100 metres below. The cape is barren and there is very little shade: it's a wild-west setting much appreciated by film directors.

cabo espichel

WALK

Dominating the Cape complex is the **Santuario de Nossa Senhora**. Dating from 1701 and built on the site of an earlier chapel (1495), this was once the most important place of pilgrimage in Portugal, as the two arms of pilgrims' cells either side of the building testify (it was later supplanted by Our Lady of Fátima further north). The bland exterior is deceiving: the church is richly decorated inside, with a most impressive roof painting of the Assumption in *trompe l'oeil* style by Lourenço da Cunha. To protect the sanctuary — and the coast itself — forts were built in the 18th century. But the early 19th century, beginning with Napoleon, saw the onset of repeated sackings, until the Church authorities in Sintra withheld both finance

> **See also cover photograph**
> **Distance:** 11km/6.8mi; 3h
>
> **Grade:** moderate, with an overall ascent of 400m/1300ft (500m/1640ft if you descend to Praia dos Lagosteiros. You must be sure-footed and have a head for heights along the cliffs — and keep away from the edge, especially on windy days! *IGE 1:25,000 M888 Series map, sheet 464*
>
> **Equipment:** see pages 14-15; binoculars for viewing dinosaur prints
>
> **Transport:** 🚍 from Lisbon to Setúbal then Seisimbra as on page 85. From there Carris 🚍 3205 runs to the Cape, departing 08.30 and 12.25 daily. Last bus back from the Cape leaves at 17.40 daily. Or 🚗 to/from Cabo Espichel, where there is a large car park (38° 25.180'N, 9 12.798'W)
>
> **Refreshments en route:**
> I Love Espichel café-restaurant at the sanctuary, Lobo do Mar in Seisimbra for ultra-fresh fish
>
> **Opening times/prices:**
> **Santuario de Nossa Senhora** daily except Wed from 10.00-13.30 and from 14.30-17.00; free entry

and the sanctuary's sacred effigy of the Virgin. With changing attitudes towards the religion and the monarchy, Portugal became a republic in 1910, after which the complex fell into ruin.

walk & eat LISBON

cabo espichel **walk 9**

Aerial view of the pilgrimage complex. In 1964-65 private money from the Gulbenkian Foundation began the long work of restoration. The church and 'hostels' take centre stage (there has been talk of creating an hotel in the hostels). To the right, above the cliff called 'Pedra da Mua', is the enchanting chapel shown on page 106, the Ermita da Memória. The café I Love Espichel is at the left of the east wing. In the foreground is the 'waterhouse' (shown below) under scaffolding during its restoration. Notice in the aerial view the aqueduct running in from Azóia at the back of the building; this is how the pilgrims got their water.

walk & eat LISBON

Lighthouse rising up above the beautiful strata at Cabo Espichel

cabo espichel **walk 9**

Start the walk at the **bus stop/car park** by **Nossa Senhora do Cabo Espichel** (**O**): follow the access road back out of the complex and after 400 metres go left on a track signed for the dinosaur tracks ('Pegadas Pedra da Mua'); there is also an information board for the yellow/red-waymarked **'Maravillas do Cabo' route**, the PR2 (as well as the GR11). And indeed there *are* many 'wonders' to see on this windswept cape! You quickly cross the remains of the aqueduct which supplied the pilgrims with water.

> **150 million years of strata...**
> The photo at the left, of the lighthouse south of the church, shows the fascinating strata — dating from the late Jurassic to the Cretaceous — at the Cape, an eastern extension of the Serra da Arrábida visited on Walk 7.
> **...and dinosaur prints**
> Sure-footed walkers could slither down to Praia dos Lagosteiros to get a closer view of the Pedra da Mua dinosaur tracks dating from the late Jurassic, just below the Ermita da Memória. The less impressive Lagosteiros footprints date from the Cretaceous are more easily seen. The two sets of prints are only about 500 metres apart in distance, but 50 million years apart in time — and in completely different rock.

After 350 metres, at a fork (**1**), you come to the steep path down left to **Praia dos Lagosteiros** (**a**) — partly in an eroded rainwater channel. If you're very keen on having a closer look at the Pedra da Mua dinosaur tracks than you will have from the 'official' viewpoint, take this detour — remembering that it will add over 100m of re-ascent (very tiring on a hot day).

The main walk keeps straight on here. At the next fork, after 60 metres, go left, heading along the edge of the cliffs above the beach. Keep straight on at the next fork. A good view opens out

111

walk & eat LISBON

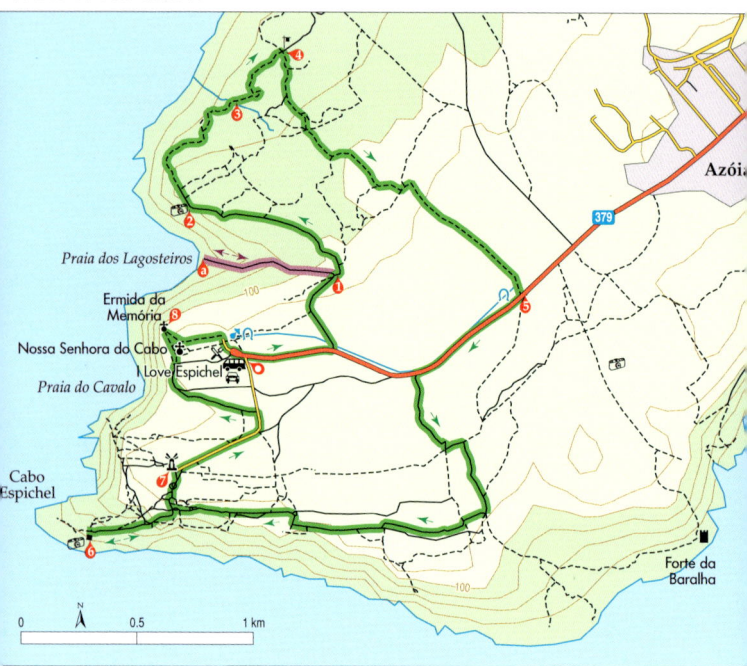

on the right to the coastline further north — on clear days you can even see to Cascais.

The wide track ends at the official **viewpoint** for both sets of dinosaur prints (❷; **17min**). Keep away from the cliff edge! The Pedra da Mua tracks are directly below the tiny white Ermita da Memória on the south side of the beach. If you are wondering how the dinosaurs *ran(!)* up the 100-metre-high cliff, they didn't. In the late Jurassic this was flat land and the sea a warm water lagoon. Later tectonic movement inclined the rock at the precipitous angle it is now.

It was due to these footprints that the present-day Ermita da Memória was built and worship of Our Lady of Cabo Espichel was promulgated. Legend has it that two elderly people from different villages dreamed of a light above the Cape. The Virgin appeared to each of them and urged them to travel there. When they met up and approached the cliffs they both saw a mule carrying the Virgin and Child up the sheer cliff — only to disappear when they entered a little chapel on the clifftop. As proof of what they had seen, they pointed out the 'mule tracks in the rock' (Pedra da Mua means 'Mule's Rock'). The current *ermita* was built not long after, at the start of the 15th century, in the same spot as the earlier place of worship.

From the viewpoint keep left and head northwest. You cross a streambed (❸; **26min**) — usually dry — then rise straight on, to a crossroads with a **signpost** (❹; **43min**). Turn right here

You walk behind the church on your way to the Ermita da Memória

The Cape is only barren at first glance — it can be a riot of colour

with the PR2, leaving the GR11 to head off left. At a T-junction 40 metres further on, turn right, then go straight on.

At the end of a slight ascent, go left at a waymarked fork and carry straight on following the PR2 for 1km (a tiny pine wood provides some welcome shade on a hot day) to the **Azóia-Espichel road**. Here you turn right (**5**; **1h20min**); 150 metres along are very substantial remains of the aqueduct. (You could shorten the walk by just going back to the start now.)

The main walk used to turn left here for 200 metres, then follow a track down to the one of the old ruined forts, the Forte da Baralha. This used to be PR1, but in the meantime part of the land has been sold and it there is now a 'Propriedade privada' sign at the start of the track. So follow the road to the left for some 500 metres, then turn left down an eroded track.

Stay on this wide, obvious track which after about 300 metres makes a 90° turn to the left and then heads back to the right, downhill, again — narrowing eventually to become a cart track. After about 400 metres turn right on another track. At this point it doesn't matter which track you follow as long as you keep parallel with the road above, heading towards the lighthouse on Cabo Espichel.

About 1400 metres along, at a crossroads of tracks, turn *left* — to the old **naval base and lighthouse** (125m; **6**; **2h30min**). There are fine views of the Cape and sea from the graffiti-splattered stone benches by the old gun emplacements.

Then go back to the fork and turn left to the beautiful lighthouse (**7**; **2h40min**). Its 1000-watt bulb lights up the sky for about 45km! Then make your way behind the church, to the lovely **Ermita da Memória** (**8**); it's locked, but if you peek in through the glass door you can see some lovely *azulejos;* one depicts the Virgin on her donkey, climbing the steep Pedra da Mua. From here make your way back to the sanctuary of **Nossa Senhora do Cabo** (**O**; **3h**).

I Love Espichel

What may have started as a simple café is now a very popular café-restaurant, with excellent reviews — and plenty of (rather poor quality) photos on their Facebook page of the restaurant itself — and their super meals! The building is at the left, behind the cross, in the photo on pages 108-109.

Grilled prawns at I Love Espichel

I LOVE ESPICHEL
Cabo Espichel (21 268 5628
daily, except Wednesday,
from 09.00-20.00 €-€€

specialities include this platter of **fried prawns** (*camarão frito travessa*), fried **cuttlefish** (*choco frito*), **bacalhau** with cream, **seafood platters** featuring prawns, brown crab, clams and limpets with various sauces.

regional desserts and quite an array of **cocktails** (see their web pages!)

The menu changes every day, so there is no guarantee that all the specialities listed above will be on offer. While fish and seafood make up the major part of the menu, there *is* usually a meat dish every day. As well as lunch, they also serve very hearty snacks (*petiscos*) — like Portuguese meats and cheeses or *bacalhau* fritters — as well as a choice of hearty sandwiches like the spicy *Francesinha* (a toasted roll with roast meat, cheese and an ale sauce).

restaurants
eat

Drunken pears *(peras bebadas)*

It isn't often that a 'café' — especially one in 'in the middle of nowhere' — serves pears in red wine! It's hard enough to find this elegant party-stopper even in upmarket restaurants.

Slice the vanilla pod legthways and remove the black seeds. Place the pod in a large saucepan together with the sugar, cinnamon and wine. Completely immerse the peeled pears and cook for 20-30 minutes, until soft.

Leave the pears in the liquid and chill. They can be left like this for a day to allow the flavour to really soak into the pears.

Finally, remove the pears and boil the liquid down to about half, reducing it to a syrup. Allow the syrup to cool.

Serve the pears with the syrup, a piece of cinnamon stick and a sprig of fresh mint.

Although it is most common in Portugal to serve the pears on their own, this truly international dish goes well with cheese boards, with roasted meats or — obviously — with vanilla ice cream!

Ingredients (for 4 people)
4 whole peeled pears with stalks remaining (Portuguese rocha pears for preference)
1 vanilla pod
1 bottle red wine (one of the rich red wines from the Alentejo works well)
225 g caster sugar
1 cinnamon stick
fresh mint

Lourinhã's fame is due largely to the significant palaeontological finds in the Jurassic limestones that outcrop along the nearby coastal cliffs. Palaeontology and the Jurassic conjure up visions of dinosaurs, and almost everywhere in the town you will see references to the fossil remains found locally.

lourinhã's dinosaurs
WALK

lourinhã's dinosaurs **walk 10**

Lourinhã lies some 65km/ 40mi north of Lisbon, just inland from the coast. The town itself is pleasant and has the atmosphere of a bustling centre for the local agricultural industry. This walk takes you from Lourinhã town centre (after a visit to the excellent dinosaur exhibits in the museum) out to the coast and then northwards past the fine sands of Praia Areia Branca to the coastal fort of Pai Mogo, where fossil dinosaur eggs have been found.

Distance: 8.7km/5.4mi; 1h54min (one way)

Grade: easy-moderate, with an overall ascent of about 150m/500ft. Mostly good paths, **very poorly** waymarked. One or two short, steep gradients. *IGE 1:25,000 M888 Series map, sheet 349*

Equipment: see pages 14-15

Transport: Rodoviária Rápida Azul 🚌 786 from Lisbon (Campo Grande, not on the plan, on the north side of the city, with metro station) to Lourinhã. Departs Lisbon hourly on the hour from 08.00; weekdays (only at 10.00 weekends); departs Lourinhã at 15.55, 17.10, 18.40 weekdays (only at 16.25 weekends); journey time 1h. Website: rodoviariadooeste.pt. Prearrange a Lourinhã taxi (see page 125) to collect you from the Forte de Paimogo viewpoint for the return!

Refreshments en route: cafés, restaurants in Lourinhã (start of the walk) and Praia da Areia Branca (see page 126)

The bus station is quite close to the old town centre of **Lourinhã**. First walk to the museum: turn right as you come out of the bus station and, at the roundabout, take the second left exit (Rua Miguel Bombarda, with a brown sign to the 'Biblioteca Municipal'). Soon you come into a small square (Praça Marquês de Pombal); leave this by following Rua 5 de Outubro. At a T-junction which comes up immediately, turn right. Now the **Lourinhã Museum** is just 30 metres along to your left.

walk & eat LISBON

Cleaning fossils in Lourinhã's museum and Lourinhã's Gothic church

The museum has various sections, including a good display focussing on traditional agriculture. There is also an exceptionally well displayed and documented exhibition of dinosaur fossils, many collected locally from the route of this walk. You can either visit the museum now or when you return to Lourinhã; either way, it's not to be missed!

Our walk proper starts from the front of the **museum** (18m; (⭕)). Be warned: it used to be well signposted and waymarked, but not any longer! Refer to the map or our GPS tracks, since most of the signs are missing and the waymarks have all faded. With your back to the museum's entrance, turn left and take the second left turn, by the Café Central, along Rua da Misericordia (brown sign 'Igreja do Castelo', as well as a fingerpost for the **PR1** walk to Forte de Paimogo). Walk round to the left of the 16th-century church, the **Igreja do Castelo** (**2min**), noting its

simple Gothic line. Then continue down the tarmac lane from the main entrance of the church, passing the **cemetery** off left. Cross a road and continue straight ahead downhill on a gravel road (**5min**) which crosses a smelly stream a minute later.

Just over the stream you emerge on a road, where you turn right. At a T-junction with another road (**7min**), turn right again, and follow this road to another T-junction (**10min**). Turn left, following the road for under 200 metres, then turn left off the tarmac onto a dirt road (❶; **12min**). This track starts rising gently as you pass through an area of orchards sheltered with high cane windbreaks (**14min**). Three minutes later the track swings right and levels off, then starts climbing again. Turn right at a T-junction, then cross a road (where you may see a fingerpost for 'Lourinhã'; **31min**) and continue ahead. The road rises past some old **windmills** off to the left.

At the top of the hill (90m; **35min**) the dirt road levels off, and in another two minutes you come out to a T-junction with a tarmac road and sea views ahead. In the spring the fields here are bordered by swathes of yellow *Oxalis pes-caprea* which, although very pretty, is regarded by the farmers as a problem weed. Turn right at the T-junction, and the road will lead you into the hamlet of **Casal Labrusque** (❷; **40min**).

Continue on the main road through the houses until the road starts to descend (**44min**), at which point you turn left on Travessa do Moinho (just in front of a tiled sign wishing you 'Boa Viagem'). Turn right at a fork almost at once, towards a windmill; 50 metres further on, turn left on Rua Moinho just beyond the windmill (❸; **Moinho do Roque**). Now you have

lourinhã's dinosaurs walk 10

Walking through the orchards north of Lourinhã

some fine views down to Praia da Areia Branca. The tarmac ends and a dirt track comes under foot (**46min**); you might spot some waymarks on wooden posts here.

Follow the track as it swings to the right, between high cane windbreaks. Look out for the tiny, delicate purple flowers of *Fumaria officinalis* which can be found along the wayside in this area. The dirt track becomes sandy and reduces to a trail (**53min**), as you drop down towards the beach.

Cross the parking area for **Praia da Areia Branca** (**59min**) and keep ahead to a **boardwalk** and **bridge** over the **Rio Grande** (❹; **1h08min**). You find yourself just below Foz, a bar-café/restaurant. If you continue along the beach you will find steps up onto the small promenade just a couple of minutes beyond the restaurant (our lunch suggestion; see overleaf).

Continue north along the promenade until you are led up to the right of the youth hostel (**Pousada de Juventude**; **1h15min**). Turn left at the Y-fork after the hostel, walking up the road (fingerpost; Estrada de Paimogo) past the housing developments of the **Praia da Areia Branca** urbanisation. Still on the road, you reach the top of the rise (**1h22min**), and the road starts to descend. Three minutes downhill, a rough track turns off to the left (**1h25min**); it leads to **Praia Vale de Frades** (❺; **1h27min**), if you fancy a swim.

The walk used to carry straight on from the beach on a track, then path to the next beach. But a major landslip on this headland (**Ponta de Vale de Frades**) a few years ago wiped out both track and buildings. So if you took this beach detour, return to the tarmac Estrada de Paimogo — in fact a very attractive road with a watercourse either side and cane windbreaks. Some 800 metres beyond the Praia Vale de Frades track, turn left off the road at a vehicle lay-by (**1h40min**), following a small footpath which leads down towards the next beach. Take care, a minute after leaving the road, to turn *right* by a fingerpost (which doesn't indicate which way to go!). *Be careful too, if the ground is wet;* the marly soil here can be slippery.

You descend to a small stream at the bottom of the valley,

just above the next beach, **Praia do Caniçal** (**6**; **1h44min**). You now join a wide dirt track which takes you up onto the next headland (**1h48min**). At the top you rejoin the tarmac road and turn left. Follow the road until you can take a footpath off left to **Forte de Paimogo** (44m; **7**; **1h54min**). The fort dates from 1674 and was one of a line of coastal defences set up between Peniche to the north down to the Tagus in the south. It was also intended to protect the easy landing offered by the beach at Areia Branca from seaborne invaders. The fort has remained largely unaltered since it was built. It was being restored at press date, but one wonders how it will even *survive* the coastal erosion that is causing constant landslips on this headland — a headland of considerable geological interest, being the site where the dinosaur eggs displayed in Lourinhã Museum were discovered. Dinosaur footprints have also been found in the vicinity.

At the bottom of the road there is a VIEWPOINT (**8**), and further along, partway down the stone-laid lane to **Praia de Paimogo**, there used to be a small restaurant. But it has been closed for several years, damaged by another major landslip.

If you haven't pre-arranged a taxi, use your mobile to call one from Lourinhã now (℡ 261 321 816, 917 262 803, 910 172 972). You may be able to have another swim while you wait — this is a very pleasant, uncrowded beach. And if you come in the 'season', there should be a bar restaurant open on the beach.

Alternatively, retrace your steps to Lourinhã — a total walking time of just under four hours without stops (almost 17km).

Foz

This bar-café and restaurant's appeal is not only in the food, but the incredible feeling of being a part of the sea, sand and sky as you enjoy your meal perched on the end of a rocky outcrop right on the beach, watching the surfers. The menu offers a wide range of dishes, from light meals and snacks to hearty Portuguese fare.

Caldeirada de peixe as served at Foz; opposite: assembling the ingredients at home

FOZ
Praia da Areia Branca, Lourinhã
(261 469 348
daily ex Thursdays, lunch and dinner €€–€€€

Selections from the *regional menu*:

light meals, including omelettes and sandwiches

speciality is locally-caught **fish** and **shellfish** — simply grilled or incorporated into traditional dishes like *caldeirada de peixe* (a fish stew, see recipe opposite)

selection of **grilled meats**, including steak, pork chops and veal cutlets

restaurants

eat

Fish stew
(caldeirada de peixe)

In the bottom of a heavy-based saucepan put the finely sliced onion rings and chopped garlic cloves. On top of this put the sliced potatoes, strips of red pepper and chopped tomatoes (skinned and seeds removed).

Tear the bay leaf and add together with the finely chopped coriander and wine. Season with the olive oil, pepper and sweet paprika. Cover and cook, occasionally shaking the pan, do not stir.

Cut the fish into large pieces and, when the potatoes are nearly cooked, add the fish and shellfish in alternate layers. Season with salt and continue cooking until the fish and shellfish are ready.

Serve from the same saucepan, ensuring everyone has a portion of all the layers. Top with fried bread (optional).

Ingredients (for 4 people)

- 1.5 kg of mixed fish
- 500 g prawns (or other types of shellfish)
- 2 onions, finely sliced
- 2 cloves of garlic, chopped
- 1 red pepper, in strips
- 450 g ripe tomatoes, chopped
- 500 g potatoes, finely sliced
- 200 ml white wine
- 1 tbsp olive oil
- 1 bay leaf
- 2 tsp sweet paprika
- 1 bunch of coriander, finely chopped
- salt and pepper
- 4 slices of fried bread (optional)

Today Alcochete's pleasantly sleepy atmosphere belies its past importance as a favourite hunting ground for kings João I and II. However, its history goes back much further, as it was apparently a centre for the production of domestic ceramics in Roman times, making use of the locally abundant water, wood, clay and sand.

alcochete

EXCURSION

From 17th century the town became an important producer of salt (the old flats are still visible), and a significant local fishing industry also developed. Many of the buildings in the town date from this period. These industries both declined from the mid-20th century, and Alcochete increasingly became a backwater as new communication links to the south bypassed it.

But Alcochete suddenly leapt back into prominence with the building of the new Vasco da Gama bridge, not least because the bridge impinged on the Tagus Estuary Natural Reserve, an internationally recognised bird sanctuary. The bridge won.

With the new bridge and improved fluvial links, the town is rapidly becoming a dormitory for Lisbon. To date, this has not spoilt its pleasant mid 50s atmosphere.

Leaving Seixalinho, a ferry terminal on the south side of the river, ask the taxi driver to drop you at **Alcochete's tourist office** *(turismo)*, which is quite central. Pick up a map of the town, then just spend some time looking around the narrow

Transport: from the Estação Fluvial at Terreiro do Paço (south of the Praça do Comércio) to Seixalinho (*not* Seixal); half-hourly departures; crossing takes 20min. Then taxi from the terminal to Alcochete (20min; approx €13.50). For the return there are regular buses back to Lisbon from Avenida Revolução 86 (www.carrismetropolitana.pt); journey time 30min to the Estação Oriente at the Parque das Nações (see page 38). (The same website has buses from Seixalinho to Alcochete.)

Refreshments: at Alcochete (see page 131)

Opening hours:
Park office, Tagus Estuary Natural Reserve: weekdays 09.30-13.00; 14.00-17.30; (212 348 021

Area map: see page 134

Bright tiles decorate some houses on a street in Alcochete

streets, with rows of typical fishermen's houses, the simple lines of the church and the pretty little central square where, almost certainly, you will find the male population of the town holding their daily 'parliament'.

Do call in at the **Centro Interpretação** for the **Reserva Natural do Estuário do Tejo** (closed on weekends). Established in 1976, the reserve covers over 14,000 hectares, has a resident population of flamingoes and attracts huge populations of migratory species, including half the European population of wintering avocets. Happily, the 'marriage' of bridge and bird life does not seem to have been too unfortunate. Ask at the office for information on guided walks in the protected area.

There are plenty of local restaurants to choose from in Alcochete but, if you would like to try something different, we recommend the **Restaurante Solar do Peixe** (closed Wednesdays), which is opposite 'Turismo' and facing the Tagus estuary. This restaurant serves a fish stew called *cataplana de tamboril* (*cataplana* of monkfish).

Cataplana de tamboril at the Restaurante Solar do Peixe, showing the clips of the cooking vessel

The *cataplana* is a cooking utensil that is in the shape of two metal hemispheres that seal together using two clips. The *cataplana* is used on the top of the hob, and can be turned over to achieve even cooking. This method of cooking is traditionally from the Algarve, but is now used throughout Portugal.

If you prefer a simpler and more 'typical' restaurant, try **O Alcochetano** just next door (closed Mondays); this restaurant has plenty of grilled fresh fish and seafood.

In the centre of the town there is **O Cantinho do Ti-Tonho** (closed for dinner Monday and Tuesday), another restaurant with a 'típico' ambience and *fado* sessions on Sunday and Thursday evenings.

Our final recommendation is **Os Petiscos do António** (closed Tuesdays) in Largo Barão Samora Correia — a small pleasant restaurant offering Portuguese cuisine.

Óbidos was designated a National Monument in 1951. Just one look on arrival tells you why: it is an almost perfectly preserved medieval town, totally enclosed in the still-complete walls and topped off with a delightful little castle. You enter the town beneath this beautiful tiled gateway.

óbidos

EXCURSION 2

Óbidos is, deservedly, an extremely popular day trip destination from Lisbon, so it is easy to join one of the many guided tours on offer.

> **Transport:** Rodoviária Rápida Verde 🚍 788 from Lisbon (Campo Grande, see page 119 under 'Transport' for location and website) to Óbidos. Departs Lisbon hourly on the hour from 07.00; departs Óbidos hourly at 15min past the hour from 12.15; journey time 1h.
> **Refreshments:** at Óbidos (see page 135)

But it is less expensive and more fun to 'do your own thing' by going there on the very good bus service, and then wander around (and have lunch!) at your own pace, following your own interests.

Even better, if you are able to, spend a night there (the charming castle is nowadays a *pousada*) and then have time to explore this delightful town after the day trippers have gone, or before they arrive the next day.

You will find the **tourist office** just by the **bus terminal**. They have plenty of literature in English which will help you make up your own guided tour — you can even hire an audio guide for the day.

As you walk into the town from the bus terminal you will immediately be greeted with the town gate (**Porta da Vila**) shown opposite. This was the main access to the town from about 1380, when Óbidos was located on the coast (the silting up of the Rial Estuary in the 16th century created the Lagoa da Óbidos and has stranded the town some 11km inland). The gate shelters an oratory dedicated to the town's patron saint, Nossa Senhora da Piedade (17C) and has a remarkable tile covering dating from 1740-1745.

walk & eat LISBON

restaurants • **óbidos**

Óbidos: church of São Pedro; chicken, *nouvelle cuisine*-style, at 6 Rua Padre Nunes Tavares

Within the city walls of medieval Vila de Óbidos there are plenty of restaurants to choose from. But tucked away in the shelter of the wall itself was a restaurant offering typical regional Portuguese food in a '*nouvelle cuisine*' style, the restaurant of the hotel **Casa das Senhoras Rainhas** at 6, Rua Padre Nunes Tavares. It has had several different names, but always the same telephone: ℭ 262 955 360. In summer you can eat outside on a patio beside the old walls. The restaurant (open daily) has a menu in English and takes credit cards.

Just *outside* the city walls, in Rua Porta do Vale, is the **Restaurante A Nova Casa de Ramiro** (ℭ 967 265 945; closed Sundays and Monday lunchtime) — No 1 on Trip Advisor. This restaurant has a wonderful medieval atmosphere. The décor is soft and subdued, with rich ochre pastel-coloured walls and ceiling. There is row of four huge storage pots along one wall, and the old kitchen fireplace gives added warmth to the place. The food doesn't disappoint either: we highly recommend the roast kid and turbot kebab.

restaurants
eat

BACALHAU

Bacalhau is such a fundamental ingredient in Portuguese cooking that no book claiming to feature Portuguese food could possibly avoid including at least one recipe for the famous codfish.

Every Portuguese housewife knows from childhood and parental tuition how to choose, prepare and cook the salted, dried cod. In fact each of these three steps is crucial to the success or failure of the final dish. One thing is certain: indifferently prepared, poor-quality *bacalhau* will give truly awful results! Good quality, well prepared *bacalhau* is a completely different story — immediately enjoyable, even to the non-Portuguese.

Selection

To the visitor, the piles of different qualities, prices, origins, etc can be totally bewildering. You will usually find some or all of the following qualities for sale:

Corrente (average)
Crescido (a bit better)
Graúdo (substantially better)
Especial ('special' — top quality)
Asa Branca
Cura Amarela

The first four are ranked in order of quality, starting with the basic. *Asa Branca* means that the dark inner lining of the 'wings' has been removed. The final designation means smoked. This obviously results in a very much stronger flavour — probably too strong for most foreign palettes.

recipes

eat

Traditionally, *bacalhau* came from the Grand Banks off Newfoundland. Today most comes from Norway. The Portuguese will tell you that the best quality of all these days is from Iceland.

Whichever quality you select to use, the fish should be dry and hard.

Bacalhau — a bewildering selection

Preparation

This is almost as important as the initial selection. The key is to rehydrate the flesh and remove the salt. This takes time. You will need to soak the fish for *at least* 24 hours, with several changes of water. Some recommend that the soaking be done under flowing water; others suggest that towards the end of the soaking process the fish should be put in milk for a final period of soaking, to further soften the flavour. After that, depending on the dish you are preparing, you will have to skin and bone the fish.

The quick way

These days you can avoid much of the above hassle (but miss the fun!) by buying ready-prepared *bacalhau* in the supermarket. This is called *bacalhau molhada*. It is sometimes found on the fish counter, or may be available frozen. It still has to be soaked, but for less time (as explained on the packets). At least all the skinning and de-boning has been done.

As we mention on page 9, one of Sunflower's requests was for us to search out wheat-, gluten- and dairy-free dishes. Food intolerances are becoming ever more common, and even for those who have learned to cope at home, it can be daunting to go on holiday. Rest assured that gf-df eating is very enjoyable around the Mediterranean and in Portugal, where olive oil, fish, tomatoes and 'alternative' grains and flours are basic to the diet. Many, many dishes are *naturally* gluten- and dairy-free.

EATING IN RESTAURANTS

The most common **first courses** are soup, fish and salads. Beware of *soups;* many are bread-based *(açordas).* **Main courses** in this region feature fish and seafood, especially grilled, steaks, chops and roasts. Sauces *(molhos)* usually consist of wine, tomatoes, onions, herbs and garlic, all reduced rather than thickened with wheat flour (as you can see from our recipes). If you are a sauce addict, it is safer to *ask* (see inside back flap for help in Portuguese, although the staff usually speak English). *Fried* fish is invariably dusted with flour (otherwise it is more difficult to cook), but *ask:* they may be happy to do it for you without flour. All our recommended restaurants cook meals individually; the staff are always accessible. For **sweets**, try the gf, df Molotov pudding (page 43) or orange roll (page 91). All restaurants offer fruit (including many 'exotics'); some have gf, df chocolate dishes (made with dark chocolate); *ask!*

SELF-CATERING

While many hotels in Lisbon can cater for food intolerances — or will let you use their fridges (just label your container), consider self-catering (see page 14), so that you can try some of our recipes with the *authentic local* ingredients.

Gf, df shopping

Most of the large supermarkets have a 'Natural Food', section but the choice may be limited. So make for **Celeiro** in the Baixa area (27 on the plan), where you will find a very wide range of gf, df, vegetarian, vegan, macrobiotic and organic foods. Founded in 1974, Celeiro now has a chain of 13 shops; they can, for instance, be found in most of the 'commercial centres'), but the one in Baixa is the best stocked.

The Baixa branch also has a **self-service restaurant**, open Mon-Fri during store hours, and, while the main emphasis is on vegetarian and vegan dishes, there is also a good selection for the gf, df diet. Menus are changed daily and even posted on their website! Unfortunately it is only in Portuguese at present.

CELEIRO
Rua 1º de Dezembro, 65
(main branch); ✆ 210 306 030/31/32
www.celeiro.pt
open Mon-Fri 08.30-20.00,
Sat 08.30-19.00

Schär breads, pastas, biscuits, flours, cakes; also many other gf purveyors not known in the UK — a great opportunity to sample new things!

Provamel soya drinks, sweets, cream, margarine

MENU DECODER

sopa soup
- sopa de legumes vegetable soup
- sopa de marisco seafood soup

peixe fish
- amêijoas cockles
- atum tuna
- bacalhau dried codfish
- camarão prawns
- carapaus horse-mackerel
- cherne turbot
- dourada dory
- enguia eel
- gambas giant prawns
- lagosta crayfish
- langueirôes razor shell
- lavagante lobster
- linguado sole
- lulas squid
- marisco shellfish
- mexilhões mussels
- pargo sea-bream
- peixe-espada swordfish
- percebes barnacles
- pescada whiting
- polvo octopus
- robalo sea-bass
- rodovalho halibut
- salmão salmon
- salmonete red mullet
- sapateira crab
- sardinhas sardines
- tamboril monkfish
- truta trout

carne meat*
- borrego lamb
- carne de vaca beef
- cabrito kid
- coelho rabbit
- faisão pheasant
- fígado liver
- frango chicken
- leitão suckling-pig
- pato duck
- peru turkey
- porco pork
- vitela veal

*cuts of meat
- costeletas cutlets, chops
- lombo loin, sirloin
- bife beefsteak, steak

*cooking methods
- assado roast/baked
- churrasco barbecued
- cozido boiled
- espetada kebab
- estufado braised
- frito fried
- grelhado grilled
- guisado stewed
- na brasa grilled on hot coals
- recheado stuffed

salada salad and legumes vegetables
- abacate avocado
- alface lettuce
- alho garlic
- batatas potatoes
- cebola onion
- cenoura carrot
- cogumelos mushrooms
- couve cabbage
- ervilhas peas
- espinafres spinach
- feijão beans
- pepino cucumber
- pimento capsicum pepper
- tomate tomato

fruta fruit
- ananas/abacaxi pineapple
- banana banana
- laranja orange
- limão lemon
- maça apple
- melão/meloa melon
- morangos strawberries
- pêra pear
- pêssego peach
- uvas grapes

other menu items
- açucar sugar
- azeite olive oil
- azeitonas olives
- gelado ice-cream
- leite milk
- manteiga butter
- paté paté
- pão bread
- pimenta pepper
- piri-piri hot pepper sauce
- presunto smoked ham
- queijo cheese
- sal salt
- vinagre vinegar

GLOSSARY

glossary

SHOPPING ITEMS (for fish, meat, fruit and vegetables see menu decoder)

bacon *toucinho*
basil *manjerico*
bay (leaves) *louro (em folhas)*
beer *cerveja*
biscuits *bolachas*
bread *pão*
butter *manteiga*
cake *bolo*
cheese *queijo*
cider *sidra*
cinnamon *canela*
coffee *café*
coriander *coentros*
cream *natas*
curry powder *caril*
eggs *ovos*
flour (wheat) *farinha de trigo*
maize flour *farinha de milho*
corn flour *amido de milho*
fruit juice *sumo*
garlic *alho*
ham
  cooked *fiambre*
  smoked *presunto*
herbs *ervas*
honey *mel*
ice cream *gelado*
lard *banha*
milk *leite*
coconut milk *leite de côco*
mustard *mostarda*
nuts *nozes*
olive oil *aziete*
olives *azeitonas*
paprika (sweet) *colorau doce*
parsley *salsa*
pâté *pâté*
pepper *pimenta*
pepper (red) paste *massa de pimentão*
rice *arroz*
salt *sal*
sausage *salsicha*
  pork/flour *alheira (farinheira)*
spicy *chouriço*
soup *sopa*
soya *soja*
spaghetti *esparguete*
spices, condiments *condimentos*
sugar *açucar*
tea *chá*
vinegar *vinagre*
wine *vinho*
  red *tinto*
  white *branco*
water *água*
  still *sem gás*
  sparkling *com gás*

CONVERSION TABLES

Weights		Volume		Oven temperatures		
10 g	1/2 oz	15 ml	1 tbsp	°C	°F	gas mark
25 g	1 oz	55 ml	2 fl oz	140°C	275°F	1
50 g	2 oz	75 ml	3 fl oz	150°C	300°F	2
110 g	4 oz	150 ml	1/4 pt	170°C	325°F	3
200 g	7 oz	275 ml	1/2 pt	180°C	350°F	4
350 g	12 oz	570 ml	1 pt	190°C	375°F	5
450 g	1 lb	1 l	1-3/4 pt	200°C	400°F	6
700 g	1 lb 8 oz	1.5 l	2-1/2 pt	220°C	425°F	7
900 g	2 lb			230°C	430°F	8
1.35 g	3 lb			240°C	475°F	9

Transport

The best way to get to Sintra from Lisbon is by **train** from Rossio station (nearest metro: Restauradores). The service runs half-hourly Mon-Fri, hourly on weekends. Journey time is 30min. There is also a daily hourly service on Mira/Sintra/Meleças trains: change at Benfica for Sintra. For all information go to www.cp.pt. From Sintra station it is a good half-kilometre walk to the old centre, so you may prefer to jump on a Scott URB Hop-on, hop-off bus.

The Scott URB Hop-on, hop-off card costs 12.50, is valid for 24 hours and provides transport between all the major tourist sites in Sintra.

Suburban services from Sintra have been taken over by Carris Metropolitana (carrismetropolitana.pt). Their website is in English, with route profiles and bus stops. Not all their buses begin at Sintra railway station, so it is wise to check boarding points in advance and arrive early. At time of writing tickets are sold on the bus itself, not online.

index of places and recipes

bold type: photograph; *italic type:* map

PLACES
Adraga **74**, 76, 79
Alcochete **128**, 129, **131**
Azenhas do Mar **62,** 64, **66**
Azóia 56, 60
Cabo da Roca **58**, 76, 81
Cabo Espichel **106**, 107, **108-9**, **110**, 111, *112*, **113**, **114**, 115, **cover**
Capuchos Monastery 48, **49**
Comporta 94, **95**
  Museu do Arroz **100**
Ericeira 107, *108*
Lisbon
  Alfama 25
  Belém 28, **29**
  Castelo S Jorge 23, **24**
  Mercado da Ribeira **18**, 31
  Parque das Nações **4**, **28**
  Praça do Comércio **27**
  Rossio 21
  Santa Luzia **23**
Lourinhã 119, *121*
Lourinhã museum 119, **120**
Monserrate Palace **47**, 48, **50**
natural parks
  Arrábida 85
  Sado 97
  Tejo 129, 130
Óbidos **132**, 133, **135**
Pai Mogo, Fort *121*, 125
Peninha **54**, 55, 56
Praia da Areia Branca **118**, *121*, 124
Praia da Ursa 76, **80**
Praia das Maçãs 64, 67, 75
Praia Grande 64, 69, 76, **77**
Sado Estuary 87, 93, 94
São Luís, Serra de 85, 86, **88**
Setúbal **85,** 89, 90
Sintra 35, 37, **41**
  Cruz Alta *36*, 40
  Moors' Castle **34**, *36*, 39, 42
  Pena Palace, *36*, 39, **40**
Várzea de Colares 63, 64, **65**, 70
Zambujal **109**, 111

RECIPES
cakes
  queijadas de Sintra **42**
desserts
  drunken pears **117**
  leite-creme **33**
  orange roll **91**
  sweet rice pudding **103**
fish
  dried cod Brásstyle **32**
  dried cod, selection and preparation **136**
  fish stew **127,** 131
  marinated horse mackerel **53**
  rodizio de peixe **90**, 91
  turbot and prawn kebab **61**
meat
  pork with clams **83**
  rabbit stew **73**
poultry
  chicken stuffed with spinach and nuts **52**
  duck rice **104**
rice **99**, **102**, **103**, **104**
seafood
  clams Bulhão Pato-style **105**
  Goan-style curry **44**
  razor-shell and cockle rice **102**
soup
  açorda Alentejana **45**
  prawn and bread soup **73**
wine 11, 12, **68**
  pears in red wine **117**

walk & eat LISBON

Third edition © 2025
Published by Sunflower Books
PO Box 36061, London SW7 3WS
www.sunflowerbooks.co.uk

All rights reserved. No part of this publication may be reproduced, stored in a retrieval system, or transmitted by any form or by any means, electronic, mechanical, photocopying, recording or otherwise, without the prior written permission of the publishers.

ISBN 978-1-85691-566-3

Cover photograph: Ponte 25 de Abril across the Tagus

Photographs: pages 106-117 and cover: Shutterstock; page 88 Ricardo.moniz, CC BY-SA 4.0, via Wikimedia Commons; all others Paul Burton
Maps: Nick Hill for Sunflower Books. Base map data © OpenStreetMap contributors. Contour data made available under ODbL (opendata commons.org/licenses/odbl/1.0)
Cookery editor: Marina Bayliss
A CIP catalogue record for this book is available from the British Library.
Printed and bound in the UK by Short Run Press, Exeter

Before you go ...
log on to
www.sunflowerbooks.co.uk
and click on the '**updates**' tab for walk & eat around Lisbon, to see if we have been notified of any changes to the routes or restaurants.

When you return ...
do let us know if any routes have changed because of road-building, storm damage or the like. Have any of our restaurants closed — or any new ones opened *on the route of the walk?* (Not Lisbon restaurants, please; these books are not intended to be complete restaurant guides!)
Send your comments to info@sunflowerbooks.co.uk